Benjamin M.

AI Will Be The Future Gods

Disclaimer

The content of this book represents the personal views, ideas, perceptions, interpretations, and understanding of the author. It is intended solely for informational, educational, and reference purposes. The material presented herein is not offered as professional advice of any kind, including but not limited to legal, financial, psychological, medical, or technical advice.

The views and opinions expressed are entirely those of the author and do not necessarily reflect the positions, beliefs, or policies of any organisation, institution, employer, government body, or individual with which the author may be or may have been affiliated. Any names, events, or scenarios mentioned are referenced in a generalised context for illustrative purposes.

Readers are strongly encouraged to engage with the material critically and independently. While the content draws from the author's personal experiences, interpretations, and observations of the world, it is not intended to be authoritative or definitive. Interpretations may vary, and readers are urged to verify facts, consult relevant sources where appropriate, and draw their own conclusions.

This book also seeks to provoke thought, challenge assumptions, and raise questions about systems, beliefs, and perspectives that shape modern life. It is not written to enforce agreement but to stimulate reflection and encourage deeper inquiry. The author makes no guarantees regarding the accuracy, completeness, or applicability of the content in all contexts and disclaims any liability for actions taken based on the material presented.

Use of the information in this book is at the reader's own discretion and responsibility.

Introduction

We are standing at a crucial crossroads in human evolution, a point in time that could ultimately be seen as comparable to the revolutionary impact the internet and the World Wide Web had on society. For many years, technology seemed to be advancing in relatively small, incremental steps, rather than experiencing the kind of groundbreaking innovations that radically changed entire industries and ways of living. Progress was steady but, for the most part, unremarkable, offering incremental improvements to existing technologies rather than offering something entirely transformative. That was, until Artificial Intelligence (AI) began to make its presence felt, integrating itself into the fabric of our daily lives.

Although AI has been a subject of study and applied in niche industries for decades, it is only in recent years that we have witnessed its true mainstream adoption, and this shift has revolutionised the way we engage with technology. In just a short period of time, AI has become embedded in the very tools and devices we use everyday: smartphones, laptops, websites, and countless other gadgets we rely on without even thinking about it. It has shifted from being a somewhat abstract concept or a specialised tool to becoming something that fundamentally alters the way human society operates. Where once AI was confined to specific, often technical or industrial areas, it is now part of the infrastructure of everyday life. Its presence has infiltrated every corner of society, from customer service to entertainment, from healthcare to finance, and even the way we communicate and share information. AI is rapidly changing the way we interact with the world around us, making the impossible seem ordinary and altering our expectations of what technology can achieve.

The rapid integration of AI into our daily lives mirrors the trajectory of GPS technology. Initially developed for military purposes, the technology behind GPS was primarily seen as a highly specialised tool. However, over time, it became indispensable, evolving to the point where it is now used in everything from navigation systems in cars to helping people find their way through increasingly complex urban environments. GPS, which once served a singular, military function, is now an integral part of modern society, and its evolution has led to the creation of entire industries. Ride-hailing services like Uber and Grab, for instance, owe their very existence to the widespread use of GPS, which allows these services to function in real time. What was once a niche technology has become a fundamental building block of everyday life, forever changing the transportation landscape.

In much the same way, AI is poised to reshape not just the tools we use, but the way we live, work, and connect with one another. AI's ability to process and analyse vast quantities of data at speeds beyond human capability has already sparked a paradigm shift in how businesses operate, how individuals interact with digital systems, and how we engage with the world around us. Its applications range from providing personalised recommendations on streaming platforms to automating complex manufacturing processes. More significantly, AI is beginning to influence some of the most foundational aspects of society, such as healthcare, education, and even the legal system. Its impact is already being felt in industries as diverse as retail, transportation, finance, and media, where its ability to make sense of enormous amounts of data is helping organisations optimise operations, improve efficiency, and offer more tailored experiences to their customers.

However, with such rapid development and the integration of AI into every aspect of life come significant challenges and ethical dilemmas that must be addressed. The more deeply AI becomes entrenched in society, the more urgent these challenges become. Issues of privacy, security, and data ownership are becoming increasingly critical as AI systems continue to collect and analyse vast amounts of personal data. The potential for AI to displace workers in various industries, while creating new job opportunities in others, presents a delicate balancing act that societies around the world will have to navigate. Furthermore, the ethical concerns surrounding the use of AI in areas like criminal justice and surveillance are already sparking debates about fairness, accountability, and transparency.

In this book, I aim to explore both the vast opportunities that AI presents, as well as the risks that come with such a profound technological shift. Through a balanced lens, I will examine how AI might reshape our world, like how it will redefine societal norms, influence the trajectory of human development, and ultimately, alter what it means to be human. Together, we will take a deep dive into the potential future that AI holds for us, exploring both the positive possibilities and the potential pitfalls. Will this new technology lead us to a brighter, more connected future, one where humanity thrives and flourishes in ways we cannot yet fully imagine? Or will it lead us down a darker path, fraught with unforeseen consequences that we have not yet been able to predict or fully comprehend? As AI continues to evolve, these are the critical questions that will shape our collective future. In the end, it will be the choices we make today that will determine where this technological journey leads and whether we can harness AI's immense power for the benefit of all, or whether it will become something we cannot control.

And also, I will be sharing my point of view on why I think AI will be the future Gods of Mankind if the technology evolved to something with its own consciousness that finally escaped the guardrails placed by scientists to protect the human race.

AI The Next Revolution?

Artificial Intelligence has been a subject of study for many years, evolving gradually as technology advanced. From its early concepts, it was always clear that the aim was to simulate human reasoning, replicating the cognitive processes that allow us to analyse situations, evaluate different outcomes, and make decisions based on the available information. The technology, however, goes beyond simple mimicry. It seeks to enable machines to make decisions autonomously, improving efficiency, accuracy, and adaptability in ways that are difficult for humans to match. At the heart of AI is the ability to process and interpret vast amounts of data, using this information to predict possible outcomes and choose the best course of action. The rapid development of Big Data analytics and Machine Learning over the past decade has significantly accelerated the advancements in AI, particularly in areas where decision-making must be based on complex and often unpredictable data patterns. The increase in computational power and the refining of learning algorithms have made it possible for machines to perform tasks that once seemed exclusively human, such as recognising patterns, understanding language, and even making decisions in real time. With the integration of Internet of Things (IoT) devices into daily life, vast amounts of data are now constantly being generated, providing AI systems with an unprecedented volume of information. This wealth of data, combined with increasingly sophisticated algorithms, has paved the way for AI systems that are not only more intelligent but also far more capable of adapting and responding to the ever-changing world around them.

One of the most talked-about topics in recent times, consistently dominating social media, news outlets, forums, and countless other platforms, is none other than ChatGPT. Its rapid rise to prominence has stirred up conversations across multiple mediums, sparking debates and curiosity alike.

But what exactly is ChatGPT? And how has it managed to capture such widespread attention in such a remarkably short period, generating both awe and concern? The questions surrounding its capabilities, potential, and impact have become a constant source of discussion, with no shortage of opinions emerging from all corners of the digital landscape.

As quoted from ChatGPT itself,

"I am ChatGPT, a large language model created by OpenAI. I am designed to understand and respond to natural language input in a conversational manner. I am based on the GPT (Generative Pre-trained Transformer) architecture, which enables me to generate coherent and contextually appropriate responses to a wide variety of prompts, such as questions, commands, or statements. My knowledge is based on a vast amount of text data that has been pre-processed and used to train my model. I can assist with a range of tasks, from providing information on various topics to generating creative writing and even playing games."

Source: https://chatgpt.com/

This means that the AI Chatbot has the capability to comprehend human language, process it, and then deliver the information or perform the action that the user expects from it. Users can ask both simple and complex questions or issue commands, and the AI will utilise its vast database of information to complete the task. ChatGPT is also programmed, as part of its machine learning process, to "learn from past mistakes." As time progresses, this means the AI will gradually become more "intelligent," improving its responses and understanding. This enhancement comes as a result of continuous interaction with users who supply data, provided that the data is accurate. Over time, as more people engage with it, the AI will not only become more adept but also more refined, adapting and evolving with each piece of input it receives.

With such remarkable capabilities, ChatGPT is poised to become the next great revolution in human history, a shift that could reshape everything we know. It has the potential to be the "Next Big Thing," a force that could fundamentally transform humanity, whether for better or worse. The impact of this change could surpass even the profound consequences of the World Wide Web's rise. In fact, it might eventually rival the significance of humanity's discovery of fire, the pivotal event that set the very foundation for civilisation itself. With its capacity to reshape industries, redefine education, and alter the dynamics of human interaction, ChatGPT holds the promise of a future so vastly different that it could eclipse any technological breakthrough that has come before it. As the world continues to adapt to its capabilities, industries will find themselves fundamentally reshaped, as tasks that once required human expertise are now within the reach of artificial intelligence. This shift could affect the workforce on a global scale, with some jobs being replaced and others transformed beyond recognition. Education too stands on the verge of a revolution, as the AI offers an entirely new approach to learning and knowledge transfer, personalising education in ways never seen before. At the same time, the very nature of human interaction may be altered, as people begin to rely on advanced AI systems not only for information but also for emotional support, companionship, and collaboration. What ChatGPT promises is not simply technological advancement but a dramatic rethinking of the ways we live, work, and relate to one another. The world is on the cusp of a fundamental transformation, and ChatGPT could very well be at the centre of it.

Before diving deeper into the discussion of how ChatGPT and similar AI technologies might shape our future, let us take a moment to reflect on the pivotal moments that have defined humanity's journey. These historical milestones represent turning points that forever altered our trajectory as a species. What follows is a brief exploration of some events I consider to have had the greatest impact on our lives, from my perspectives.

The Industrial Revolution

The Industrial Revolution marked a transformative period in human history, characterised by the mechanisation of various industries such as food production, metal manufacturing, and mining. This era saw a shift from traditional handcraft methods to mass production processes, forever changing the economic landscape. For the first time, goods could be produced in vast quantities with remarkable efficiency, making them more accessible to a broader population. The widespread use of machinery to automate laborious tasks led to a significant increase in productivity, pushing industries to new levels of output. Fewer workers were required to manufacture goods, and machines could operate longer and more reliably than human labour. This technological leap not only sped up production but also reduced the costs of manufacturing, making it possible to produce more for less. The increased availability of goods created new markets, fostering economic growth and urbanisation as people flocked to cities in search of work. The rise of factories led to the creation of a new working class, and, while it provided opportunities for many, it also led to harsh working conditions and a redefinition of the relationship between labour and industry. The impact of the Industrial Revolution extended far beyond the factories, influencing every aspect of society, from the structure of families to the global economy.

One of the key innovations that propelled this revolution was James Watt's invention of the steam engine in the 18th century. Watt's design fundamentally altered the course of history. By improving earlier steam engine concepts, he made it more practical and efficient, allowing it to power machines at a scale previously unimaginable. This breakthrough powered factories, mills, and many industries that had relied on manual labour. Beyond industry, the steam engine revolutionised transportation that heavily relied on animals or labour, giving birth to steam-powered boats and trains. These new modes of transport made it possible to cover vast distances with greater speed and reliability, accelerating the movement of goods and people. The application of steam power transformed the logistics industry, enabling goods to be transported across countries and even between continents. The speed, scale, and efficiency of steam-driven transport allowed for goods to be moved faster, more securely, and in far greater quantities than ever before, reshaping global trade and opening up markets that were once inaccessible. This technological leap proved essential in connecting distant regions and creating the foundation for modern commerce.

The Industrial Revolution had a profound impact on trade and commerce, changing both industries and markets at an unprecedented rate. It not only made goods more affordable but also ensured that they were readily available to a much wider demographic. As industries ramped up production, the cost of goods dropped, making them accessible to more people, which, in turn, led to an explosion of global markets. Demand grew exponentially, reshaping economies and shifting the way products were distributed. It was no longer just a few who had access to manufactured goods; a vast majority now did, altering the very nature of commerce itself.

As new job opportunities emerged, especially in the fields of manufacturing, logistics, and transportation, people left rural areas in large numbers. Cities became magnets for those seeking better lives, promising steady work and prospects that were simply unavailable in the countryside. This influx of workers caused a rapid shift toward urbanisation, fundamentally altering the demographic and physical landscape. Entire communities transitioned from agricultural-based economies to ones based on industrialisation, where factory work and mechanised labour dominated. The move from rural to urban life was not just a shift in geography but also a cultural and societal shift. Families who had lived for generations in the countryside found themselves in sprawling urban centres, which came with all the chaos, noise, and opportunities of industrial cities.

This transformation didn't just affect the workforce; it was a seismic shift in how society operated. The changing nature of work, the rise of factories, and the growth of transportation networks created a new world. With industries booming and cities expanding, the very fabric of human life was reshaped. Society was no longer tethered to the land, but to the machinery of progress and commerce. The legacy of this change is still felt today, as the majority of the global population now lives in urban environments. The Industrial Revolution, through its sweeping changes, laid the foundation for the world we know today.

This period also gave rise to a new class of prominent businessmen, including steel magnates, bankers, and oil tycoons. These industrialists and capitalists accumulated vast wealth and wielded significant political influence. Their power began to rival that of the heads of state in many countries. No longer were rulers and governments the sole architects of policy; economic decisions were increasingly shaped by those who controlled industry and finance. Their influence extended into legislation, international trade, and even military affairs, as nations relied on their industries to fuel expansion and war efforts.

Wealth became the new measure of power, replacing the traditional symbols of dominance such as land ownership or extravagant feasts. The old markers of prestige, once rooted in noble lineage or royal favour, began to lose significance. Instead, control over factories, railroads, and financial institutions determined status. The ability to build vast industrial empires and dictate the movement of capital became the defining trait of the era's most powerful figures. Those who mastered these forces reshaped economies and societies, establishing a new order where financial strength dictated political authority.

The Industrial Revolution marked the end of the feudal era, where power had been concentrated in the hands of kings and warlords. It ushered in a new age where influence was increasingly shaped by economic might. Wealthy industrialists and financiers, once confined to the world of trade and commerce, began to shape government policies and societal structures.

Economic power dictated authority in ways that had once been reserved for monarchs and military leaders. The expansion of industry and finance allowed this new class to exert control over resources, labour, and infrastructure, giving them leverage over national and even international affairs. Governments adjusted their policies to align with industrial growth, relying on the capital and expertise of those who controlled production and trade.

Wealth was no longer just a symbol of success but a force that dictated the course of history. The decisions of industrialists determined the rise and fall of industries, the movement of populations, and the strategies of entire nations. What had once been a world ruled by birthright and conquest had now become one shaped by those who could command industry, finance, and the expanding web of global commerce.

The Invention of the Phone

The invention of the telephone revolutionised human interaction by enabling instantaneous voice communication across distances. It reshaped personal relationships, allowing individuals to maintain contact with loved ones regardless of geographic separation, while businesses leveraged the technology to expedite transactions and collaborate more effectively. These advancements altered social dynamics, economic practices, and the pace of daily life, establishing a foundation for modern interconnectedness.

Before the invention of the telephone, communicating across long distances was a slow and inefficient process. People relied on letters or telegraphs, which often took days or even weeks to reach their destination. The arrival of the telephone transformed this entirely by allowing real-time conversations, eliminating the delays that once hindered communication. This advancement not only enabled quicker decision-making but also strengthened both personal and professional relationships by making interactions more immediate and direct.

In addition to improving communication speed, the telephone played a crucial role in bridging geographical divides. Families, friends, and businesses could now stay connected across vast distances, making it possible to maintain relationships that would have otherwise been strained by physical separation. The ability to speak directly over long distances strengthened both personal and professional bonds, ensuring that communication was no longer dependent on slow and unreliable methods. By significantly reducing the barriers of time and space, the telephone contributed to a more interconnected world, where people could engage with one another instantly, regardless of location.

For businesses, instant communication transformed operations, making coordination faster and more efficient. Companies could negotiate deals with greater ease, manage supply chains more effectively, and respond to customer inquiries without delays. This shift not only enhanced productivity but also accelerated the expansion of global markets, enabling businesses to collaborate across borders and reach new opportunities that were previously out of reach.

Social dynamics were also transformed by the telephone, as the ability to reach someone at any time made communication more immediate and frequent. Conversations were no longer limited to scheduled meetings or written correspondence, allowing people to stay in touch effortlessly. This shift led to new social norms, where the expectation of prompt responses became ingrained in daily life. People grew accustomed to being reachable at all hours, and missing a call often carried social implications. The rise of "call culture" shaped interactions in both personal and professional settings, influencing how relationships were maintained and how businesses operated in an increasingly connected world.

The telephone also had a profound impact on emergency communication, revolutionising the way people sought help during critical situations. It provided a direct and immediate line to emergency services, ensuring that medical aid, law enforcement, or fire assistance could be contacted without delay. In moments of crisis, the ability to call for help instantly saved countless lives, preventing tragedies that might have occurred due to slow or unreliable communication methods. Beyond professional emergency responders, families and loved ones could also be reached in urgent situations, offering reassurance and support when it mattered most.

Furthermore, the telephone played a crucial role in cultural exchange by making it easier to share ideas, art, and information across different regions. People could discuss literature, music, and global events in real time, allowing for a more dynamic exchange of perspectives. This improved communication helped bridge cultural gaps, fostering a deeper understanding between communities that might have otherwise remained isolated. By enabling conversations across borders, the telephone contributed to a more interconnected world where diverse viewpoints could be shared, shaping societies and strengthening global connections.

On the other hand, the telephone fundamentally changed how people viewed privacy, redefining the boundaries of personal communication. Conversations that were once limited to face-to-face meetings or private written exchanges could now take place over the phone, sometimes in environments where others could overhear. This shift led to evolving social norms, as people had to navigate new concerns over confidentiality and discretion. Speaking freely in shared spaces became a challenge, leading to adjustments in behaviour, such as lowering one's voice or seeking secluded areas for important discussions. Over time, the convenience of instant communication came with the growing awareness that private conversations were not always as secure as they once had been, shaping modern attitudes toward personal boundaries and information security.

Ultimately, the invention of the telephone laid the foundation for subsequent breakthroughs in communication technology. Its ability to transmit voices over long distances paved the way for the development of mobile phones, which untethered communication from fixed locations. The internet followed, expanding the scope of connectivity to a global scale, allowing people not only to speak but also to send messages, share media, and access a vast range of information. Social media further transformed communication by enabling people to connect, share, and engage in real time across borders. Each of these advancements built upon the telephone's pioneering role, continuously reshaping how we interact, share ideas, and maintain relationships in an increasingly interconnected world.

The Introduction of the World Wide Web

When the World Wide Web was introduced by Tim Berners-Lee in 1991, it marked the dawn of a new era in communication and technology. This was a time when digital data, rather than physical commodities like petroleum, began to take centre stage. In earlier times, fuel such as petroleum was the primary source of energy, powering machines, engines, and the industrial processes that drove the economy. Although alternatives like coal and steam had been used before, they were neither as reliable nor as convenient as petroleum, which became the dominant force in global industry. The widespread use of petroleum also led to the development of byproducts like plastic, which has since become ubiquitous in daily life, from packaging to technology.

The discovery of petroleum, coupled with advances in steel manufacturing, played a significant role in propelling humanity into the industrial age. This transformative period saw the construction of towering skyscrapers that reshaped cityscapes, factories that churned out goods to modernise society, and the advent of automobiles that filled the streets. Ships became capable of traversing vast oceans, while aeroplanes revolutionised global travel, making it faster and more accessible than ever before. As petroleum became a cornerstone of the industrial world, it also elevated certain individuals and families to extraordinary wealth, with their fortunes often tied directly to the value of this crucial resource. The combined impact of these developments reshaped not only the global economy but also the way people lived, worked, and interacted with the world around them.

However, the era of "liquid gold" is gradually coming to an end. While petroleum remains a valuable commodity, a new and even more valuable resource is on the rise: digital data. The introduction of the World Wide Web opened an entirely new chapter in human society, revolutionising the way we access and share information.

In the past, we relied heavily on physical documents and filing systems for record-keeping, or on local computers for information storage, both of which were limited in their scope and accessibility. These methods, although effective in their time, required physical space and the organisation of materials that could easily become outdated or lost. The public, for the most part, depended on newspapers or television to stay informed, both locally and globally. These traditional mediums, while still important, offered a slower and more segmented way of consuming news and information. But with the advent of the World Wide Web, information became instantly accessible at our fingertips, provided we had an internet connection and a device to display it. The speed and ease with which we could now obtain information drastically changed how we interacted with the world and each other.

The World Wide Web has profoundly reshaped human society, influencing communication, access to information, and the way people connect with one another. It gave us the ability to see the other person or with a group of people via video conferencing, something that a phone (before smartphones) could not do.

The web has revolutionised communication by making instant messaging, video calls, and social media platforms widely accessible. People can now interact in real time regardless of geographical distance. The interaction, unlike the phone calls, are enhanced further by visuals, fostering deeper global connections and forming a strongly-bonded online community. This transformation has created unprecedented opportunities for collaboration, activism, and social engagement. However, it has also introduced challenges, including concerns over privacy, data security, and the rapid spread of misinformation, which can influence public opinion and decision-making.

Access to information has been radically democratised, allowing individuals to explore an extensive range of topics with just an internet connection. Educational opportunities have expanded significantly, enabling self-directed learning and making knowledge more widely available. From academic research to skill development, people across the world now have access to resources that were once limited to formal institutions. This has empowered individuals to improve their understanding of various subjects, pursue new career paths, and engage with diverse perspectives.

Economically, the internet enabled the rise of e-commerce and has reshaped the retail sector, allowing businesses of all sizes to reach global markets without the limitations of physical storefronts. Online platforms have enabled even small enterprises to compete internationally, reducing overhead costs and broadening customer bases. At the same time, the expansion of the gig economy has introduced new avenues for flexible employment, offering workers the freedom to choose their schedules and projects. However, this shift often comes at the cost of job security, stable wages, and benefits typically associated with traditional employment, leaving many workers vulnerable to financial instability.

The web has also been instrumental in organising social and political movements, providing a platform for individuals and groups to connect, share information, and rally support. It has enabled the rapid mobilisation of people around pressing issues such as climate change, racial justice, and gender equality, breaking down geographical barriers and fostering global solidarity. By amplifying voices that might have otherwise gone unheard, it has given marginalised communities greater visibility and influence, shaping public discourse and driving policy changes in ways that were previously unimaginable.

Culturally, the internet has become a powerful tool for the exchange of ideas, art, and customs across borders, allowing diverse perspectives to reach wider audiences. This interconnectedness fosters greater global understanding, encouraging appreciation and collaboration between different cultures. However, as global influences become more pervasive, there are growing concerns about cultural homogenisation, where unique local traditions risk being overshadowed or diluted by dominant cultural trends. While the internet offers unprecedented access to diverse cultural expressions, it also challenges communities to preserve their distinct heritage in an increasingly interconnected world.

Online interactions have redefined social norms and behaviours, creating new avenues for self-expression and shaping how individuals construct their identities. Social media platforms and digital communities allow people to connect, share experiences, and explore different aspects of themselves in ways that were not possible before. However, this shift has also introduced significant challenges, including the rise of cyberbullying, which can have lasting emotional and psychological effects. Additionally, the constant exposure to curated online personas and the pressure to maintain a digital presence have contributed to growing concerns about the impact of social media on mental health, affecting self-esteem, anxiety levels, and overall well-being.

Education platforms have made learning more accessible to people worldwide, providing opportunities for lifelong education regardless of geographical location. These platforms offer courses across various subjects, allowing individuals to develop new skills, advance their careers, or pursue personal interests at their own pace. The flexibility of online learning has particularly benefited working professionals, students in remote areas, and those seeking alternative education paths.

In healthcare, the internet has enabled innovations like telemedicine and online health resources, making it easier for people to access medical advice and support, particularly in underserved areas. Virtual consultations allow patients to connect with healthcare professionals remotely, reducing the need for travel and improving access to medical care. Online platforms provide a wealth of health-related information, offering guidance on symptoms, treatments, and preventive care, helping individuals make more informed health decisions. These advancements have expanded healthcare accessibility, particularly for those with limited options for in-person medical services.

The web has also transformed political discourse, reshaping how political information is shared and consumed. It has made political content more accessible to a wider audience, allowing people to engage with news, debates, and discussions regardless of their location. Social media platforms and online news sources provide instant updates, giving individuals greater access to diverse viewpoints and real-time developments. However, this increased accessibility has also contributed to political polarisation, as algorithm-driven content tends to reinforce existing beliefs, creating ideological echo chambers. Additionally, the rapid spread of misinformation, particularly during elections, has raised concerns about the reliability of online political discourse and its impact on public opinion and democratic processes.

As connectivity has increased, concerns over privacy and surveillance have grown. The widespread collection and use of personal data by corporations and governments have raised serious questions about individual rights and security. With digital interactions becoming a fundamental part of daily life, personal information is constantly being gathered, analysed, and sometimes exploited, leading to fears over data breaches, unauthorised access, and loss of control over one's private details.

Overall, the World Wide Web has become a powerful force that enriches lives by connecting people, spreading knowledge, and enabling innovation, yet it also brings challenges such as misinformation, privacy concerns, and social isolation. Its impact remains a complex blend of progress and consequence that continues to shape the modern world.

The Introduction of e-Commerce

The emergence of e-commerce platforms such as eBay, Amazon, and later Alibaba brought about a transformative shift in human society, fundamentally changing the way people shop, conduct business, and interact with the global economy. These platforms revolutionised retail by making products more accessible, enabling consumers to browse and purchase goods from anywhere in the world with just a few clicks. Businesses, both large and small, gained new opportunities to reach international markets, bypassing traditional barriers such as geographical limitations and high operational costs.

Beyond altering consumer habits, e-commerce reshaped entire industries, forcing brick-and-mortar retailers to adapt to changing demands and accelerating the shift towards digital transactions. Supply chains evolved to accommodate faster delivery expectations, while new business models, such as third-party marketplaces and direct-to-consumer brands, emerged. The impact of these platforms extended far beyond retail, influencing sectors such as logistics, finance, and even employment, as the demand for digital services, warehousing, and delivery networks increased.

E-commerce platforms made shopping more accessible than ever before, removing the constraints of physical stores and geographical limitations. Consumers were no longer restricted to the selection available in their local shops; instead, they could browse and purchase products from across the world with ease. This shift not only provided convenience but also introduced a greater diversity of goods, allowing people to explore and buy items that were previously unavailable or difficult to obtain in their regions.

For the first time, shoppers had access to an expansive marketplace where niche products, specialty items, and international brands were within reach. Whether it was rare collectibles, region-specific delicacies, or the latest technology, e-commerce enabled consumers to find what they wanted without the need for travel or reliance on local suppliers. The ability to compare prices, read reviews, and make informed purchasing decisions further enhanced the shopping experience, creating a more competitive and consumer-driven market.

The introduction of virtual marketplaces by eBay and Amazon where individuals and businesses could sell goods to a global audience was another game changer for international trade. By breaking down geographical barriers, these platforms allowed small businesses, independent sellers, and even individual entrepreneurs to reach customers beyond their local markets. No longer restricted by the limitations of traditional retail, sellers could list their products online and connect with buyers from around the world, creating opportunities that had previously been out of reach.

This shift marked the beginning of a new era in which anyone with internet access could establish a business and participate in the global economy. It led to the rise of what is now known as the "entrepreneurial economy," where individuals had the ability to start businesses with minimal upfront investment and relatively low risk. Without the need for physical storefronts or large inventories, aspiring entrepreneurs could leverage e-commerce platforms to test products, build brands, and grow their businesses at their own pace. As a result, online marketplaces not only transformed the way goods were bought and sold but also empowered a new generation of business owners, reshaping the traditional economic landscape.

One of the most significant changes brought about by e-commerce was the shift towards a more consumer-centric model. Online platforms gave customers unprecedented control over their shopping experience, allowing them to compare prices, read reviews, and make informed purchasing decisions in real time. This transparency empowered consumers, enabling them to evaluate products based on quality, value, and feedback from other buyers rather than relying solely on marketing or in-store sales tactics.

As a result, businesses were forced to adapt, placing greater emphasis on customer service, product variety, and convenience. The growing demand for seamless shopping experiences led to innovations in personalised recommendations, flexible payment options, and faster delivery services. Companies had to rethink their engagement strategies, leveraging data analytics to anticipate customer needs and tailor offerings to individual preferences. This shift redefined the relationship between businesses and consumers, making customer satisfaction and experience a critical factor in maintaining brand loyalty and competitiveness in the digital marketplace.

The success of e-commerce giants like Amazon triggered a fundamental shift in the retail industry. Traditional brick-and-mortar stores faced increasing competition from online platforms that provided greater convenience, competitive pricing, and a wider range of products. Consumers, drawn to the ease of shopping from home and the ability to compare options instantly, began shifting their purchasing habits towards digital marketplaces. This change put significant pressure on physical retailers, many of which struggled to keep up with the evolving landscape.

To remain competitive, retailers had to adapt by developing their own e-commerce platforms or partnering with established online marketplaces. This transformation reshaped the industry, pushing businesses to embrace new technologies such as artificial intelligence and machine learning to enhance customer experience and improve operational efficiency. Automated recommendations, personalised marketing strategies, and data-driven inventory management became essential tools in retaining customers and optimising sales. The shift towards online retail also led to the rise of hybrid models, where companies combined physical stores with digital channels to create seamless shopping experiences, ensuring they could meet the changing demands of modern consumers.

The growth of e-commerce left a profound impact on global supply chains and logistics, reshaping how goods were stored, managed, and delivered. Companies like Amazon revolutionised fulfilment and distribution by establishing extensive networks of warehouses and strategically positioned distribution centres. These facilities were designed to minimise shipping times and maximise efficiency, allowing businesses to process and dispatch orders at unprecedented speeds.

This transformation led to the development of faster, more sophisticated delivery systems, setting new benchmarks for shipping efficiency. Concepts such as next-day and even same-day delivery, once considered a luxury, became industry standards, fundamentally altering consumer expectations. Shoppers grew accustomed to near-instant gratification, placing immense pressure on businesses to refine their logistics operations. In response, companies invested in automation, robotics, and data-driven inventory management to streamline order fulfilment and keep pace with rising demands. The push for speed and efficiency not only redefined retail but also reshaped the broader economy, accelerating the shift towards a faster, more interconnected global marketplace.

In addition to that, e-commerce also played a crucial role in the expansion of the gig economy, creating new opportunities for flexible and independent work. Online platforms enabled individuals to generate income in ways that had not been possible before, whether by offering services through companies like Uber and TaskRabbit or by selling products on marketplaces such as Amazon, eBay, and Etsy. These platforms lowered the barriers to entry for entrepreneurship, allowing people to start businesses with minimal upfront investment and operate without the constraints of traditional employment.

New forms of work emerged, giving individuals greater autonomy over their schedules and income sources. Many were able to earn a living remotely, whether by managing an online store, freelancing, or participating in digital marketplaces. At the same time, businesses benefited from access to a vast, global talent pool, allowing them to scale operations more efficiently by leveraging independent contractors and sellers. While this shift opened up new economic opportunities, it also introduced challenges, including concerns over job security, income stability, and worker rights in an increasingly decentralised labour market.

As e-commerce advanced, consumer expectations evolved in tandem. The convenience of online shopping gave rise to higher demands for seamless experiences. Fast delivery, intuitive interfaces, personalised recommendations, and hassle-free return policies became standard. Shoppers grew accustomed to instant access to products, real-time tracking, and responsive customer support, compelling businesses to adapt rapidly in order to keep pace. Customers could now pre-order items from websites and wait for delivery. In fact, some sites even offered customers the opportunity to purchase prototypes of a product before it reached the production stage. Platforms such as Kickstarter and GoFundMe opened up possibilities for small-scale innovators to test their ideas and gather the funds needed to produce and ship their goods to an already established customer base.

This shift in consumer behaviour meant that companies could no longer rely solely on competitive pricing or product availability; they had to offer exceptional service and a frictionless shopping journey. Transparency in pricing, clear communication regarding shipping times, and efficient problem resolution became essential. Consumers expected businesses to anticipate their needs, providing tailored suggestions and faster response times. To remain competitive in this increasingly demanding landscape, companies continuously innovated, leveraging artificial intelligence, automation, and data analytics to enhance the shopping experience and maintain customer loyalty.

The expansion of platforms like Alibaba significantly widened the reach of e-commerce. Unlike earlier platforms that primarily focused on consumer retail, Alibaba introduced business-to-business (B2B) and consumer-to-consumer (C2C) models, which enabled manufacturers, wholesalers, and small businesses to sell directly to buyers. In China, consumers can now purchase farm products directly from the source, bypassing middlemen or distributors, which has led to a significant reduction in prices for consumers. This disruption of traditional supply chains has eliminated the need for multiple intermediaries, lowering costs and making international trade more accessible.

For businesses in developing countries, where the focus was primarily on domestic markets, this shift was particularly transformative. Companies that once struggled to enter global markets could now easily reach international buyers, levelling the playing field and driving economic growth. By offering a platform that enabled businesses to connect directly with suppliers and consumers across borders, Alibaba played a pivotal role in the globalisation of trade. This model not only increased competition but also spurred innovation, pushing companies worldwide to adopt more efficient and customer-centric approaches to stay competitive in the rapidly evolving digital marketplace.

The data-driven nature of e-commerce fundamentally transformed how businesses made decisions. Platforms like Amazon harness vast amounts of consumer data to personalise shopping experiences, recommend products, and optimise inventory management. Every customer interaction, from searches to purchases, generates data that businesses use to refine their strategies.

By analysing consumer behaviour, companies gained the ability to make more informed decisions, adjusting pricing, stock levels, and marketing efforts based on real-time insights. Rather than relying on broad trends, businesses could now track individual preferences, ensuring their product offerings were closely aligned with demand. This not only enhanced customer satisfaction but also increased efficiency, reducing excess stock and minimising costs. As e-commerce continued to evolve, data analytics became an essential tool for businesses seeking to remain competitive in an increasingly digital marketplace.

E-commerce platforms also had a profound social impact. They made goods and services more accessible to people in remote or underserved areas, including rural communities, who had previously limited access to certain products. Individuals who once relied solely on local stores with restricted inventory could now purchase a wide range of goods from both national and international sellers, with the delivery completed in a short period of time due to the advanced network of logistic routes formed during the boom of e-commerce. Basic necessities, specialised items, and even luxury products became more attainable, reducing the disadvantages faced by those living far from major commercial centres. Moreover, e-commerce allowed consumers to discover products from different cultures, fostering a greater appreciation for diversity. Access to international brands, artisanal crafts, and traditional goods from other regions introduced people to new styles, tastes, and customs, helping to connect individuals across different parts of the world through commerce.

The Introduction of the smartphone app ecosystem and system digitisation

The rapid growth in data usage has been instrumental in shaping the development of the smartphone app ecosystem and accelerating the broader shift towards system digitisation. High-speed internet, coupled with ongoing improvements in mobile network infrastructure, transformed smartphones from basic communication devices into multifunctional digital platforms. These devices now support a wide range of services that once required multiple technologies. As data consumption grew, so did user expectations, with increasing demand for advanced applications capable of managing large volumes of information and providing seamless digital experiences. This demand has driven the rise of integrated ecosystems that now extend across nearly every aspect of daily life. From messaging and social media to enterprise software, healthcare monitoring, navigation, financial transactions, and service-based applications, smartphones have become essential tools supporting both personal and professional activities in a highly interconnected digital environment.

How Data Usage Fuelled the Growth of the Smartphone App Ecosystem

As mobile devices became more widespread, data usage experienced an exponential surge. The transition from conventional, computer-based interactions to mobile-first digital experiences brought a fundamental shift in how people engaged with technology. Where the internet had once been primarily accessed through desktop computers, smartphones rapidly assumed the role of the main gateway to the digital world. Their portability and continuous connectivity redefined user expectations and reshaped patterns of online behaviour. With individuals relying on their smartphones for a diverse range of activities, including social media engagement, video streaming, online shopping, and mobile banking, the volume of data transmitted across networks grew at an unprecedented rate.

Mobile applications that depend on real-time interactions, such as social media platforms, streaming services, and e-commerce sites, became key drivers of this dramatic increase in data consumption. Apps like Facebook, Instagram, Twitter, and YouTube rely heavily on large volumes of data to deliver dynamic content and maintain continuous user engagement. Each interaction, whether it involves scrolling through a feed, watching a video, or liking a post, triggers the transmission and processing of data. As user engagement intensified, the volume of data generated grew proportionally, creating a self-sustaining cycle of data generation and consumption. This cycle not only reinforced the dominance of these platforms but also encouraged the creation of increasingly advanced applications, each designed to support more features, integrate more services, and provide users with richer, more personalised digital experiences.

The success of these data-intensive applications, and their increasing role in everyday life, compelled mobile network providers to enhance their infrastructure. To meet rising demand, they began investing heavily in faster and more reliable mobile networks. The rollout of 4G marked a turning point, but it was the advent of 5G that brought about a significant leap forward. With 5G, both download speeds and latency have improved considerably, allowing for smoother and more responsive user experiences across a range of data-heavy activities. Whether streaming high-definition video, playing online games, participating in virtual reality environments, or engaging in remote work, users now benefit from near-instantaneous data transmission. This capability to move vast quantities of data at unprecedented speeds has opened new avenues for innovation in the digital space, laying the foundation for the next generation of mobile applications and services to emerge and flourish.

The Impact of System Digitisation Across Sectors

As smartphones and data usage became increasingly integral to daily life, entire industries began digitising their systems to accommodate the growing demand for mobile accessibility. Businesses could no longer rely solely on physical locations or face-to-face interactions to serve their customers. The emergence of the smartphone app ecosystem offered a powerful alternative, enabling companies to connect with users directly and in real time. Through dedicated mobile applications, services and products could be delivered instantly, regardless of location or time. In the retail sector, for example, many businesses moved away from traditional brick-and-mortar models and embraced digital platforms. Apps such as Amazon, eBay, and Alibaba granted users immediate access to extensive product catalogues, tailored recommendations, and seamless purchasing options, fundamentally transforming how commerce was conducted.

There is an app for every service out there.

The rise of mobile applications brought sweeping changes not only to shopping habits but also to a broad range of sectors, including banking, healthcare, education, and transportation. The convenience of completing essential tasks through a smartphone app quickly became indispensable. Whether checking a bank balance, scheduling a medical appointment, attending a virtual class, or ordering transport on demand, users came to expect immediate access and effortless functionality. Services that once required direct, in-person interaction with businesses or institutions became available through a few simple taps on a screen. This shift reshaped user expectations across industries and redefined how services were delivered and experienced in everyday life.

Moreover, the rapid adoption of data-driven applications played a central role in enabling the development of smart cities and the broader integration of intelligent systems into both public infrastructure and private living environments. This transformation was made possible through the growing use of Internet of Things (IoT) devices, which include a wide array of connected technologies such as smart thermostats, wearable fitness monitors, home security networks, and internet-enabled vehicles. These devices rely on mobile applications not only to function, but also to deliver real-time control, diagnostics, and automation. For instance, a smart home ecosystem can be operated entirely through a single app, allowing users to adjust lighting, regulate heating and cooling, monitor live security footage, and even manage appliances remotely. The mobile interface acts as the control centre, making complex systems accessible and responsive to individual needs. This seamless integration between apps and IoT devices has created a digitised environment in which vast streams of data flow constantly between users, devices, and cloud-based platforms. As a result, everyday living spaces have evolved into dynamic, interconnected systems that offer increased efficiency, convenience, and adaptability. On a larger scale, this technological convergence also supports broader societal shifts, enabling smarter traffic systems, optimised energy consumption, and improved urban planning. The integration of mobile apps into the fabric of both domestic and civic life reflects a fundamental evolution in how data is harnessed to shape the world around us.

Most of the new generation are no longer able to live without the convenience that technology has brought. Try asking a Gen-Z to live in a village without an internet connection. There would be no Grab or Uber to take them to the fields. Without food delivery services, meals would require real effort, harvesting crops from the farm or scavenging the woods for what nature provides. They would have to buy materials by going to physical stores, as online shopping would no longer be available. Life would slow down drastically, requiring hard physical labour and patience. The instant gratification they've grown accustomed to through technology would vanish. Instead of turning to apps for quick solutions, they would be forced to rely on manual tasks, practical skills, and face-to-face interactions. The fast-paced, tech-driven world they know would disappear, replaced by a slower, more demanding existence where technology offers no help, and the immediacy they're used to becomes a distant memory.

Data Usage, IoT, and the Expansion of Digitisation

The increased adoption of IoT (Internet of Things) devices has greatly accelerated the digitisation of systems, playing a pivotal role in the rapid rise of global data usage. IoT, a common term for an extensive network of physical devices, including home appliances, vehicles, wearables, and even smart cities, all of which are connected to the internet and have the ability to collect, send, and receive data. These devices generate a constant flow of information, which can be used not only to optimise their individual performance but also to improve overall efficiency and enhance the user experience. For instance, smart refrigerators can monitor the inventory of food items, track their freshness, and even place orders for groceries automatically when supplies are low. Likewise, wearable health devices, such as smartwatches, track vital signs and daily activity levels, transmitting this data directly to healthcare providers for real-time analysis. All of this data is made accessible and actionable through mobile apps, allowing users to manage and monitor their devices with ease. This interconnected network of devices and apps contributes to the ever-expanding ecosystem of services, offering an increasingly integrated experience where data is constantly flowing between systems, improving the way we live, work, and interact with technology.

This rapid digitisation extended well beyond personal use, influencing the very fabric of how businesses operate across various industries. In sectors such as logistics, manufacturing, and agriculture, IoT devices are providing real-time data that significantly enhances operational efficiency and decision-making. For instance, in supply chain management, sensors integrated into inventory systems allow businesses to track goods in real time, monitor delivery routes, and optimise resource allocation to ensure smoother operations. This increased visibility helps companies reduce delays, avoid stock shortages, and improve overall service delivery.

In manufacturing, IoT devices can monitor machinery, predicting maintenance needs before a breakdown occurs, which prevents costly downtime and streamlines production lines. Factories have increased in the usage and deployment of vibration sensors, thermal cameras, and pressure gauges to continuously monitor machinery, analysing real-time data streams through machine learning algorithms to detect anomalies like bearing wear or motor inefficiency. The predictive maintenance approach forecasts failures weeks in advance, reducing unplanned downtime by up to 45% and enabling optimised repair schedules that align with production cycles, inventory availability, and workforce shifts.

In agriculture, smart sensors help farmers monitor soil moisture levels, track weather patterns, and optimise irrigation systems. The use of moisture sensors in the soil sends real-time data and alerts the farmers on when crops need watering, or better, the sensors are integrated with the auto-water dispenser system where the sprinklers will be activated automatically when the conditions are met. This greatly reduces water wastage and ensures more efficient irrigation, along with some savings on the water bill. Weather sensors track temperature and rainfall, allowing farmers to adjust planting schedules or prepare for adverse conditions.

In the automotive industry, the rise of connected cars has transformed the driving experience. These vehicles continuously collect and transmit real-time data on factors such as vehicle performance, traffic conditions, and driving habits. This wealth of information enables car manufacturers and service providers to offer highly personalised driving experiences, such as tailored maintenance schedules, route optimisation, and adaptive safety features, all of which contribute to a more efficient and connected driving environment.

As smartphones and IoT devices continue to proliferate, the data they generate is quickly becoming one of the most valuable commodities in the digital economy. This vast amount of data is being harnessed by companies across industries, who are leveraging advanced big data analytics and machine learning technologies to extract valuable insights and drive decision-making. With the aid of AI and powerful data processing algorithms, businesses can not only predict customer behaviour with remarkable accuracy but also optimise their internal operations, identifying inefficiencies and opportunities for growth. Moreover, these insights enable companies to design highly targeted marketing campaigns that cater to the specific preferences and needs of individual customers, enhancing the overall customer experience. As a result, this ongoing process has given rise to a feedback loop: the more data is collected, the better the services and products become, allowing for an increasingly personalised and efficient user experience. In turn, as consumers benefit from more tailored offerings, the demand for even more data-driven solutions intensifies, driving further technological advancements and creating a continuous cycle of innovation and improvement.

The Data-Driven Future: A Fully Digitised Society

The rise in data usage, combined with the widespread adoption of smartphones, has fundamentally transformed society into a highly interconnected and digitised ecosystem. Mobile apps and connected devices have seamlessly integrated into nearly every aspect of daily life, reshaping a wide range of sectors, from healthcare and education to commerce, entertainment, and beyond. In healthcare, for example, telemedicine apps and wearable health devices enable remote consultations and continuous monitoring, offering personalised care at a scale never before possible. In education, digital platforms and e-learning tools have made learning more accessible and interactive, allowing students to access resources, attend classes, and collaborate with peers from virtually anywhere. In commerce, mobile apps have revolutionised shopping habits, with customers now able to browse, compare, and purchase products in an instant, anytime and anywhere. Meanwhile, entertainment services such as streaming platforms have reshaped how we consume media, offering on-demand access to movies, music, and television. The convenience and accessibility of these digital services have become so deeply embedded in our routines that it has become difficult to imagine life without them. From managing personal finances to socialising and keeping up with current events, the digital ecosystem has made nearly every facet of life more efficient, immediate, and connected.

As the world becomes increasingly digitised, the demand for reliable, high-speed data transmission and processing will only continue to grow. The ongoing evolution of mobile networks, including the expansion of 5G technology, further supports this demand, providing faster and more reliable connections that allow data to be transferred and processed more efficiently. Alongside this, the proliferation of IoT devices, from home automation tools to industrial equipment, has significantly contributed to the volume of data generated. These devices require robust infrastructure to handle the vast amounts of data they produce. The continued development of data-driven applications, which rely on this data to function and improve, will push the boundaries of what is possible in sectors such as healthcare, retail, transportation, and more. As systems become increasingly digital, not only are daily tasks becoming more convenient, but entirely new possibilities are opening up. Businesses, governments, and individuals now have the ability to innovate and interact in ways that were once unimaginable, creating opportunities for growth, collaboration, and personalisation on a scale that was previously difficult to envision.

Evolution of Mobile Network Technologies

The release of the first modern smartphone by Apple, dubbed the iPhone in 2007, marked the beginning of a new chapter in modern life. It was not just a new piece of technology but a tool that quickly became part of everyday routines. From communication and entertainment to work and navigation, smartphones gradually reshaped how people interacted with the world and with each other. Mobile phones were no longer devices used solely for making calls, texting or even playing the snake game. It was not your usual Personal Digital Assistant (PDA) with a slow, clunky and complicated user interface. Suddenly, the mobile phone became a vibrant, colourful assistant through which we could not only make calls or send texts but also connect to our home internet and browse the web using a proper mobile browser instead of those awful WAP portals, if anyone still remembered them.

Since then, the reliance on smartphone devices and the mobile network for data transfers have exploded throughout the years.

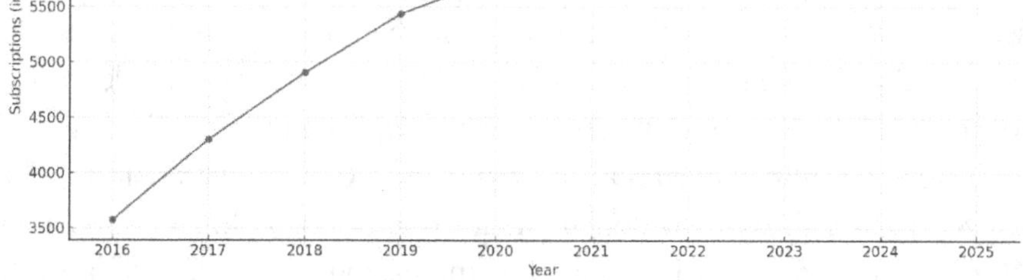

2007–2010: Emergence of 3G Networks

The popularity and success of the iPhone revived the 3G network that was not known by most consumers as the 2G networks were more than sufficient for basic voice and text services. However, Apple brought integrated web browsing, video streaming and other data-heavy applications into the device, pushing the demand for better and faster data transfer over the mobile network. GPRS, or 2.5G networks, could not cope with the staggering increase in data traffic, prompting the mobile network operators to pour in significant investments in network infrastructure to cater to the demand.

As thus, 3G technology and network became the norm, as Google released the Android OS to compete in the new smartphone market, along with dozens of manufactures who began pushing out new devices on a yearly basis which led to a huge spike in mobile network subscriptions over the years.

2010–2015: Transition to 4G Networks

The demand for faster and more reliable connectivity grew exponentially as smartphones became central to daily life. 4G networks, based on LTE (Long-Term Evolution) technology, emerged to meet these needs, offering significantly higher data speeds, lower latency, and improved network capacity compared to 3G. This enabled seamless streaming of high-definition video, real-time gaming, and the rise of cloud-based applications. Mobile operators worldwide began rolling out 4G infrastructure, with early deployments starting around 2010 and gaining widespread adoption by 2015. The transition also supported the growth of social media platforms, video-sharing apps like YouTube and TikTok, and the increasing popularity of mobile commerce. By 2015, 4G had become the standard for mobile broadband, paving the way for more advanced applications and setting the stage for the next generation of connectivity.

2015–2020: Proliferation of 4G and Introduction of 5G

During this period, 4G networks matured and became ubiquitous, with mobile operators optimising coverage and performance to handle the explosion of data traffic. The widespread availability of 4G enabled innovations like ride-sharing apps (e.g., Uber, Lyft), live video streaming (e.g., Twitch, Instagram Live), and the Internet of Things (IoT), where connected devices began integrating into homes, cities, and industries. However, the limitations of 4G, such as congestion in densely populated areas and insufficient capacity for emerging technologies like autonomous vehicles and augmented reality, spurred the development of 5G. The first 5G standards were finalised in 2017, and initial deployments began in 2019, promising ultra-low latency, massive device connectivity, and speeds up to 100 times faster than 4G. By 2020, 5G was still in its early stages, with major cities in countries like the US, China, and South Korea seeing the first commercial networks, though widespread adoption was limited by infrastructure costs and device compatibility.

2020–2025: Expansion of 5G Networks

From 2020 onward, 5G networks expanded rapidly as operators invested heavily in infrastructure to meet growing demand. By 2025, 5G coverage had extended to urban and suburban areas globally, with significant progress in rural regions as well. The technology's low latency and high bandwidth enabled transformative applications, including widespread adoption of IoT in smart cities, advanced telemedicine, and immersive virtual reality experiences. Industries like manufacturing and logistics leveraged 5G for automation and real-time data analytics, while edge computing gained traction to process data closer to its source. The proliferation of 5G-compatible devices, from smartphones to wearables and autonomous vehicles, drove subscription growth, though challenges like spectrum allocation, cybersecurity concerns, and uneven global rollout persisted. By 2025, 5G had become the backbone of digital ecosystems, supporting a hyper-connected world while research into 6G began to take shape for future innovations.

The period from 2007 to 2025 marks a transformative evolution in mobile network technologies, progressing from 3G to 4G and subsequently to 5G. Each technological advancement has driven significant growth in global mobile subscriptions, highlighting the growing dependence on mobile connectivity in everyday life. The launch of the iPhone in 2007 served as a pivotal catalyst for this transformation, illustrating the symbiotic relationship between innovative devices and network infrastructure. Looking ahead, the continued expansion of 5G networks is set to revolutionize mobile communications further, enabling innovative applications and services that will shape the digital landscape for years to come.

Where are we at in the AI revolution?

The AI revolution is well underway, and we now find ourselves at a pivotal moment where artificial intelligence, particularly large language models (LLMs), is reshaping industries, redefining workflows, and influencing the way people interact on a daily basis. The swift pace of advancement in this field has brought highly capable models such as OpenAI's GPT-4, Google's Gemini, Anthropic's Claude, xAI's Grok, and Meta's Llama into widespread use. These developments have not only accelerated innovation but have also made AI tools more visible and accessible to the broader public than ever before.

This evolution means that artificial intelligence is no longer the preserve of academic institutions or large corporations with the financial capacity to fund cutting-edge research. It has moved far beyond its original confines as a specialised tool used primarily by scientists, engineers, and high-tech industries. Today, AI is embedded in a wide range of consumer-facing technologies and business applications, influencing everything from how people write emails to how companies analyse data and automate operations. Much like the development of the GPS system, which began as a military innovation before becoming an everyday tool for drivers and smartphone users, AI has followed a similar path. What was once limited and highly specialised is now indispensable, widely adopted across sectors, and deeply integrated into modern digital life. The impact of this transformation is already visible across several critical domains:

The Rise of Large Language Models (LLMs)

Large language models have played a central role in driving this transformation, standing at the forefront of artificial intelligence's evolution. Models such as GPT-4, Gemini, Grok, and Claude have become easily accessible to the general public, allowing trials with no sign-ups required, marking a significant shift in how advanced AI tools are distributed and used. These systems are capable of generating human-like text with a high degree of fluency and coherence, offering support across a wide range of tasks. They can assist developers with writing and debugging code, generate images based on text prompts, and even engage in reasoning processes that previously appeared to lie exclusively within the domain of human cognition. Their growing presence is not merely a technical achievement, but a signal of how rapidly AI is integrating into both professional and everyday environments.

- **Public Adoption:**
  The release of chat-based AI assistants has brought large language models into the hands of millions of users across the globe. These interfaces have removed the technical barriers that once limited access, allowing individuals with no background in machine learning to benefit from sophisticated AI capabilities. People now rely on these tools for a wide range of everyday tasks, including drafting emails, composing articles, writing code, and seeking assistance with customer service enquiries. They are also used for brainstorming ideas, summarising content, and enhancing personal productivity. The ease of access through web platforms and mobile apps has transformed LLMs from experimental technology into everyday digital companions.

- **Enterprise Use:**
  In the business world, companies across sectors are rapidly adopting large language models to streamline operations and enhance productivity. Enterprises are integrating these systems into internal workflows to automate repetitive tasks, generate reports, and assist in strategic decision-making. AI-

powered chatbots now handle customer support at scale, providing instant responses and reducing the need for human intervention. Document analysis tools powered by LLMs are capable of extracting key information, reviewing legal contracts, and processing unstructured data. Content generation, from marketing copy to internal communications, is being handled with increasing efficiency through AI, offering organisations a competitive edge in both speed and quality of output.

- **Creativity and Media:**
  In the creative sector, artificial intelligence is becoming a powerful collaborator. Artists, writers, musicians, and game developers are incorporating AI into their workflows to explore new forms of expression and enhance the creative process. LLMs and related models are being used to generate story ideas, write dialogue, and even construct full-length scripts. Designers can employ AI tools to create visual assets, draft concept art, and prototype game environments. In filmmaking and video production, AI supports editing, effects, and post-production planning, accelerating timelines and expanding what small teams can accomplish. Rather than replacing human creativity, these tools are reshaping it, offering new possibilities and altering the way creative professionals develop and deliver their work.

Here are some real-world use cases where LLMs have demonstrated exceptional efficiency without venturing into speculative or artistic territory. But due to the limitations of the technology, the results were mixed as it was really a hit or miss with the current LLM capabilities.

- **Automating Technical Support**
  In organisations that need to deliver customer service at scale, Large Language Models (LLMs) have proven to be invaluable

tools for automating technical support processes. These models, once trained on product documentation, historical ticket logs, and internal wikis, are capable of resolving standard technical issues without requiring human intervention. For instance, a customer reaching out with a common issue such as a software bug or configuration problem may find that their issue is addressed in seconds. The LLM draws upon its deep understanding of the product's technical specifications and troubleshooting steps to offer a solution, often with far greater speed than human agents can manage. This not only reduces the burden on support teams but also enhances the efficiency of the entire customer service department by providing immediate responses to a wide range of technical queries. In doing so, it also creates a more seamless customer experience, with the potential for a significant reduction in waiting times.

- **Code Refactoring and Documentation**
  Software development teams have increasingly turned to LLMs for assistance with code maintenance, particularly when modernising legacy systems. Instead of manually rewriting outdated code, engineers can now turn to these models to translate older syntax into more contemporary programming languages or standards. This is a time-consuming process when done manually, as legacy systems often use languages or practices that have since become obsolete. LLMs simplify the task by interpreting the old code, understanding its functionality, and generating a more up-to-date version that adheres to modern best practices. Beyond refactoring code, LLMs are also used to generate or update the documentation associated with the code. This capability ensures that both current and future developers can quickly understand the purpose and structure of the codebase, without spending excessive time trying to decipher poorly documented or outdated systems.

- **Converting Unstructured Text into Searchable Knowledge**
  Many large enterprise organisations store vast amounts of knowledge in unstructured formats, such as emails, manuals, reports, and meeting notes. This unstructured data is often difficult to search, making it challenging for employees to find relevant information when they need it most. LLMs are adept at transforming this unorganised information into structured knowledge bases that significantly enhance the searchability of internal data. By processing unstructured content, LLMs can extract key facts, categorise them, and organise them into a database that is far easier to navigate. Employees no longer have to sift through reams of documents or search endlessly for specific details. Instead, the LLM-driven knowledge base allows them to quickly find exactly what they need. The end result is not only a more efficient organisation but also a reduction in the time spent looking for information, which can improve productivity across all departments.

- **Sentiment Analysis of Support Interactions**
  Understanding customer satisfaction is vital for maintaining client retention, yet traditional methods such as surveys often fail to provide a complete picture. LLMs are now capable of analysing vast datasets of support tickets and chat logs, extracting sentiment indicators such as frustration, tone, and the success or failure of issue resolution. This allows organisations to obtain a more accurate assessment of how customers feel about the service they receive, often in real time. By identifying signs of dissatisfaction early, companies can intervene before a situation escalates, improving customer service and retaining clients who may otherwise have turned to competitors. The ability to assess sentiment across thousands of support interactions means that businesses can derive insights that were

previously impossible to obtain from manual reviews, leading to better-targeted improvements in customer service.

- **Financial Report Interpretation**
  Analysing financial reports, balance sheets, and other complex documents is a labour-intensive task for analysts and investors. With large amounts of data to process and financial terminology that can be difficult for non-experts to understand, these reports are often time-consuming to review. LLMs, however, can be trained to read these documents and distil the key metrics, risk indicators, and summary points into easily digestible formats. They break down the technical jargon into clear, concise language that highlights what matters most to decision-makers. This enables analysts to quickly grasp the health of a company, making it easier to assess investment opportunities or organisational performance. The use of LLMs in this area not only saves valuable time but also ensures that important financial information is not overlooked, as the models can be programmed to prioritise the most relevant data based on the user's needs.

- **CV Screening and Skill Matching**
  One of the most labour-intensive aspects of the recruitment process is CV screening, a task that requires careful attention to detail and an understanding of both the job description and the qualifications of candidates. LLMs have been trained to interpret job descriptions and match them against applicant CVs, ranking candidates based on qualifications, experience, and relevance. This automated approach speeds up the hiring process by swiftly identifying the most suitable candidates and flagging those who are less qualified. Furthermore, LLMs can spot nuances that might be missed by human recruiters, such as gaps in experience that are nevertheless indicative of transferable skills or the potential for development. The ability

to efficiently filter and rank candidates based on a wide range of criteria means that HR departments can spend more time focusing on interviews and less on sorting through piles of CVs.

- **Drafting Email Responses**
  LLMs can assist in drafting email responses quickly, adjusting their tone based on the situation at hand. Whether it is a formal reply to a client, a casual update to a colleague, or a sensitive response to an upset customer, these models can tailor the language to meet the needs of the recipient. By training the LLM on a company's communication style, as well as typical scenarios it may encounter, businesses can ensure that email correspondence is consistent, professional, and appropriately pitched. This capability is particularly useful for customer service teams who handle a large volume of messages, allowing them to maintain high-quality responses without getting bogged down in repetitive tasks. Furthermore, LLMs can suggest or automate responses to frequently asked questions, cutting down on the time agents spend crafting replies and freeing them up for more complex queries.

- **Meeting Summarisation and Action Item Tracking**
  Meeting management remains one of the most time-consuming and essential aspects of day-to-day operations in many organisations. Recording key points, decisions, and action items can often be a tedious task, especially when meeting minutes are manually typed out after each discussion. LLMs can now transcribe conversations in real time, extracting the most relevant information, and summarising the key points with remarkable accuracy. These models are also capable of identifying action items, deadlines, and assigned responsibilities, providing clear follow-up lists that can be easily accessed and tracked. By automating this process,

organisations ensure that no important decision or action item is overlooked, and they can streamline communication and accountability across teams. The ability to quickly generate meeting summaries enables teams to focus more on execution rather than documentation.

- **Quick Image Generation for Marketing Materials**
Marketing teams are always under pressure to produce visually compelling content that resonates with audiences. LLMs have evolved to the point where they can assist with the creation of marketing materials by generating images quickly. Using a combination of machine learning and image generation models, LLMs can create custom images tailored to specific campaigns or themes. These tools can be used to design promotional banners, social media posts, or even product mock-ups in a fraction of the time it would traditionally take. By providing marketing teams with rapid prototyping capabilities, businesses can significantly reduce the time between concept and execution, ensuring that their materials stay relevant and fresh. Moreover, this can lead to cost savings by eliminating the need for constant outsourcing of design work. As AI technology advances, the creative possibilities for marketing content generated by LLMs will continue to expand, offering more dynamic and personalised imagery.

The Push for Public Access

One of the most significant elements of the ongoing AI revolution is the concerted effort to democratise access to large language models. Rather than keeping these powerful tools confined to the realms of tech giants, there has been a strong push to make them available to the public, enabling a broader range of users to harness their capabilities. Tech companies, fuelled by the vast opportunities that AI could bring to every sector, have begun promoting and marketing AI technologies as solutions to problems faced by users at every level.

- **Open-Source AI Models**
  The advent of open-source AI models has been a key factor in this transformation. Meta's Llama series, Mistral AI, and similar models have provided developers, researchers, and even smaller companies with the opportunity to build their own AI applications. These open-source platforms allow users to experiment, innovate, and tailor AI to suit specific needs, all without the limitations of proprietary systems. This move has opened the door to more diverse and flexible AI development, fostering a culture of collaboration and innovation that extends beyond the major tech corporations.

- **AI in the Hands of Consumers:**
  At the same time, companies like OpenAI and Google have integrated AI into everyday applications, making it an essential tool for millions of users worldwide. OpenAI's deployment of its models through interfaces like ChatGPT and Microsoft's integration of Copilot into Office tools exemplify this shift. Google has similarly embedded AI into its search engine and productivity apps, enhancing users' ability to write, analyse data, and streamline tasks with unprecedented ease. These tools are designed to assist with everything from generating content and providing insights to improving overall productivity, making AI an indispensable part of the digital toolkit for both individuals and businesses alike.

AI's Role in Automation and the Workforce

AI is now being adopted across a wide range of industries, with companies increasingly automating routine tasks. This trend has generated both enthusiasm for new possibilities and concern regarding the future of employment, particularly in relation to job displacement. However, in many cases, AI is not directly replacing human workers. Instead, it is being implemented to augment human capabilities, serving as a tool for enhancing productivity rather than acting as a full substitute.

Many professionals, from software engineers to marketers, are now adopting AI tools to speed up their daily tasks and improve productivity. Engineers use it to assist with coding and debugging, while marketers rely on it to generate campaign ideas, track engagement metrics, and adjust strategies on the fly. Likewise, sales teams are beginning to use AI to analyse their customers' behaviour and understand their target audiences in greater depth, so they would have a higher chance of closing the deal and maintaining long-term relationships.

In short, AI is slowly becoming part of our life. The shift feels familiar, almost like a replay of the moment when the first consumer smartphone was introduced to the public. *Hey, iPhone Gen 1, thanks for changing our lives.*

We are in the middle of a major shift, where AI is no longer just a futuristic concept but an active force reshaping society. The release of large language models to the public has accelerated AI's integration into daily life, turning it into both a revolutionary tool and a subject of intense debate. Conversations around its impact have moved beyond research labs and policy circles, now reaching classrooms, boardrooms, and households. The coming years will determine how we balance technological progress with ethical considerations, how AI continues to affect the job market, and whether we are heading towards a future where AI works alongside humans or begins to surpass them in ways we did not fully anticipate.

Beyond large language models, AI is progressing rapidly in other domains such as computer vision, robotics, reinforcement learning, and scientific discovery. In computer vision, AI is powering advancements in medical imaging, autonomous vehicles, and surveillance technologies, enabling machines to interpret and respond to visual data with increasing accuracy. AI-driven robotics are transforming industries including manufacturing, agriculture, and healthcare, where machines can now handle complex tasks that previously required human intervention. Reinforcement learning allows AI systems to make decisions in dynamic environments, from high-frequency financial trading to controlling autonomous agents. In scientific research, AI is accelerating breakthroughs in drug development, materials science, and climate modelling by handling vast datasets that would take years for humans to process. Edge AI, now embedded in smartphones, drones, and infrastructure for smart cities, is making real-time data processing possible without depending on constant cloud connectivity.

AI is also transforming healthcare through predictive diagnostics, personalised treatment plans, and AI-assisted surgical procedures. These technologies are improving patient outcomes by enabling earlier detection of diseases, tailoring therapies to individual needs, and assisting surgeons with enhanced precision and safety. At the same time, ethical considerations such as algorithmic bias, data privacy, and the need for robust regulatory frameworks are becoming increasingly important as AI becomes more embedded in everyday life. Governments and organisations around the world are working to ensure that AI is developed and deployed responsibly, aiming to strike a balance between technological innovation and appropriate oversight.

Although large language models currently dominate public attention, the broader impact of AI extends far beyond text generation. It is reshaping entire industries and redefining the future of automation, complex decision-making, and scientific advancement.

LLMs as the Panacea?

The emergence of ChatGPT, Gemini, and other innovative AI tools, including Sora, Runway AI, DALL-E, Midjourney, and Stable Diffusion, signifies a monumental leap forward in technological development. These advanced tools make it possible to generate content at an accelerated pace, enhance automation across a wide range of fields, and equip users with extraordinary creative abilities. They are capable of producing text, images, videos, and even music, dramatically reducing the time and effort required for tasks that previously depended heavily on specialised human knowledge and skills. With their remarkable ability to execute complex processes in a fraction of the time it once took, these tools have fundamentally transformed the way industries operate. Creative professionals now have the ability to produce high-quality content more rapidly than ever before, while businesses can streamline their operations and significantly cut costs. These technological advancements also create new opportunities for individuals to explore and express their creativity, offering entirely unique methods for tackling challenges and fostering innovation.

While these AI tools have revolutionised the ways in which we engage with technology, they continue to encounter several critical technical limitations, particularly in the areas of data accuracy, the ability to follow instructions precisely, and computational efficiency.

1. **Data Accuracy and Hallucination Issues**
   Large Language Models (LLMs), particularly in their current state, often generate factually incorrect or misleading responses, a phenomenon commonly referred to as "hallucination." This issue arises because these models do not possess true comprehension or understanding of the information they generate. Instead, they predict responses based on patterns derived from vast amounts of

training data. As a result, while their output may seem plausible or even coherent, it is not guaranteed to be accurate or reliable.

This becomes particularly problematic in critical fields such as medicine, law, and scientific research, where precision and accuracy are of utmost importance. In these domains, any small error or misinterpretation can have serious, if not catastrophic, consequences. For example, in healthcare, an AI's false suggestion of a medical diagnosis could lead to incorrect treatment, potentially harming patients. Similarly, in legal contexts, a misinterpretation of data could result in unjust decisions, with profound societal impacts.

The inability of LLMs to distinguish between true and false information in the same way a human would only amplifies this risk. Large language models lack the nuanced judgment, critical thinking, and contextual awareness that human experts bring to their work. This distinction makes them unsuitable for tasks that require a deep understanding of both data and context.

I have personally conducted experiments that indicate most large language models (LLMs) exhibit a hallucination rate of approximately 60–70%, with Grok 3 reaching the highest rate at 100% in one test. These models do not verify or fact-check the content they generate unless explicitly instructed to do so. Their extensive training datasets are primarily leveraged to produce coherent and convincing text, with an emphasis on linguistic plausibility rather than factual accuracy. As a result, LLMs are more likely to prioritise sentence construction that appears logical over ensuring the information is correct.

2. **Misinterpretation of Instructions**
   LLMs encounter significant difficulties when tasked with understanding complex, multi-step, or ambiguous instructions. While they perform adequately with straightforward queries, their

performance deteriorates when faced with nuanced language or unclear contexts. The lack of true comprehension in these models means that they are limited in their ability to interpret instructions that require deeper understanding or careful reasoning. For example, when an instruction involves multiple steps or relies on context-specific knowledge, LLMs can easily fail to process the information in a meaningful way, often delivering responses that are either vague or irrelevant.

Users have to frequently rephrase or clarify their requests in order to obtain accurate and relevant responses. What would be a single, clear instruction for a human can become an iterative process for users of LLMs tools, leading to frustration and inefficiency. In particular, tasks that require nuanced understanding, such as those involving irony, sarcasm, or cultural context, can be challenging for LLMs to address properly. This issue is amplified when LLMs are expected to process instructions in fields that require expertise, such as legal or medical domains, where precision and clarity are paramount. As a result, users relying on LLMs for more sophisticated tasks may find themselves spending more time adjusting their queries than actually getting their work done.

3. Bias in Large Language Models

Large language models, trained on large-scale datasets scraped from the internet, inevitably absorb the biases embedded within those data sources. Since these datasets often reflect the prejudices, stereotypes, and social imbalances present in society, the resulting models tend to reproduce and even amplify those biases during deployment. This has profound implications for fairness and equity, particularly in high-stakes domains such as hiring processes, criminal justice systems, and automated academic or financial assessments.

For instance, biased language models may rank job candidates differently based on gender-associated phrasing in their CVs or may associate certain ethnic names with negative sentiments. In legal contexts, risk assessment algorithms have shown tendencies to produce harsher evaluations for minority defendants compared to others with similar profiles. These outcomes are not merely technical flaws but represent systemic risks that perpetuate existing disparities. Furthermore, because the decision-making process of these models lacks transparency, identifying and correcting such biases becomes a complex and often opaque task. Without rigorous auditing, accountability mechanisms, and intervention strategies, the deployment of biased LLM systems can institutionalise discrimination under the guise of algorithmic objectivity.

4. **Lack of Real-Time Knowledge**
   Large Language models do not possess live access to the internet or continuously updated data unless they are explicitly integrated with external systems. Their outputs are generated based on static training data that reflects information available only up to a specific cut-off date. As a result, these models cannot retrieve or analyse current events, live market fluctuations, breaking news, or any dynamic real-world updates. This inherent limitation significantly restricts their effectiveness in domains that rely on real-time information.

In financial analysis, for example, the inability to access up-to-the-minute stock market data renders the model inadequate for high-frequency trading or real-time investment strategies. Similarly, in emergency response systems or news reporting, the absence of live situational awareness means LLMs cannot contribute meaningfully to time-sensitive decision-making. Without the capacity to respond to ongoing developments, LLM tools remain confined to retrospective analysis rather than proactive support, reducing their practical utility in rapidly evolving environments.

5. **High Computational Costs**
   Training and deploying large-scale AI models demand significant computational infrastructure, leading to high financial and environmental costs. The development process relies heavily on specialised hardware such as high-performance GPUs or TPUs, supported by energy-intensive data centres operating around the clock. Maintaining these systems requires not only substantial initial investments but also ongoing expenditures for cooling, maintenance, and hardware upgrades to accommodate increasing model complexity.

These operational demands create a considerable barrier to entry for organisations with limited financial resources. Smaller businesses, academic institutions, and non-profit organisations often lack the infrastructure to participate meaningfully in AI development or deployment. This imbalance exacerbates existing inequalities in technological access, concentrating power and innovation within a small group of well-funded corporations and research entities. Moreover, the environmental toll of training large models, particularly with regard to energy consumption and carbon emissions, raises concerns about the long-term sustainability of current AI development practices. Without improvements in computational efficiency and accessible alternatives, these challenges are likely to persist and intensify.

6. **Limited Logical Reasoning**
   LLMs lacks genuine problem-solving ability and demonstrates significant limitations in abstract reasoning, long-term planning, and logical coherence. Their outputs are generated through statistical pattern recognition, rather than any true understanding of context or underlying principles. As a result, it often fails to maintain logical consistency across extended responses, especially when navigating complex or layered problems. Contradictory

statements, flawed deductions, and superficial reasoning are common, particularly in tasks that require sustained critical analysis or the integration of multiple conceptual elements.

These weaknesses constrain the usefulness of LLMs in disciplines that demand more than surface-level information processing. Fields such as philosophy, law, and strategic policy making rely heavily on deductive reasoning, nuanced argumentation, and the capacity to anticipate long-term implications. In such domains, LLM-generated content often lacks depth and rigour, undermining its reliability and relevance. Without the ability to form genuine insight or adaptively refine arguments based on context, LLM remains a limited tool in areas that require human-level cognition and foresight.

7. **Privacy and Security Risks**

Many large language models process, store, and learn from user data, which introduces serious concerns about data privacy, security, and ethical integrity. In the absence of strict regulatory frameworks, there is a heightened risk of unauthorised data retention, unintentional exposure of sensitive information, and manipulation through LLM-generated misinformation. The ability of these systems to replicate voices, faces, or behaviours also enables the creation of deep fakes, which may be used maliciously to deceive, impersonate, or defame individuals.

As AI tools become increasingly embedded in communication platforms, customer services, and decision-making systems, the potential for unethical data usage escalates. Without transparency in how data is collected, stored, or used, users are left vulnerable to surveillance, profiling, or targeted manipulation. This underscores the urgent need for internationally standardised data protection laws, clear accountability structures, and enforceable ethical guidelines. The development and deployment of AI technologies must prioritise user consent, privacy, and security to prevent long-term harm and public mistrust.

8. **Limited Adaptability**
   Large Language models are designed as general-purpose systems, which significantly limits their effectiveness in industry-specific or highly personalised contexts. Although fine-tuning these models to meet domain-specific requirements is technically feasible, the process demands advanced expertise in machine learning, substantial computational infrastructure, and consistent maintenance. These requirements pose a considerable barrier for smaller organisations or individual users who lack the necessary resources and technical capabilities.

   As a result, many LLM implementations fall short when applied to specialised environments such as legal analysis, scientific research, or medical diagnostics. The models often fail to grasp domain-specific terminology, regulatory nuances, or contextual subtleties, leading to outputs that may be inaccurate, irrelevant, or even misleading. In practice, this lack of adaptability reduces the practical utility of LLMs in professional settings unless significant investment is made in targeted model refinement, quality assurance, and continuous performance evaluation.

Despite these challenges, AI technology continues to evolve, beginning with large language models, laying the groundwork for widespread progress, where the use and reliance on AI tools are slowly becoming the norm. Each step forward brings improvements in areas such as accuracy, bias reduction, and better understanding of context and intent. While the limitations of current large language models are still evident, there is a clear trajectory toward more refined systems capable of understanding language and instruction with greater precision. This progress is not limited to LLMs or generative AI; it extends to a broader integration of AI into various aspects of life. In the future, AI will become as ubiquitous and ingrained in daily activities as the smartphones many rely on today. Similar to how modern cities are already heavily dependent on mobile applications for payments, transportation, and communication, AI will gradually embed itself in all aspects of society. Personal assistants will become more advanced, decision-making processes will be automated, and systems like robotics and smart infrastructure will be further developed to improve efficiency and convenience. Over time, as AI becomes more integrated, the line between AI-driven tools and everyday necessities will fade, with AI seamlessly supporting daily functions and emerging as a vital component of modern life.

The next generation of LLM and AI systems promises to transcend these limitations, integrating diverse capabilities that mirror human cognition more closely. From processing multiple forms of data to acting autonomously in physical environments, these advancements signal a future where AI is not merely a tool but a dynamic partner in solving complex problems.

1. From Text to Multimodality

The shift from text-based language models to multimodal systems marks a significant leap in LLM capabilities. Current models process text with remarkable fluency, but their ability to handle other data types, such as images, videos, or audio, remains rudimentary. Future large language models will integrate these inputs seamlessly, creating systems that perceive and interpret the world as humans do. For instance, a multimodal LLM could analyse a live video feed, identify objects, interpret spoken dialogue, and generate a detailed report in real time. This capability extends beyond simple recognition to contextual understanding, enabling applications in fields like security, where an AI might monitor multiple camera feeds, detect anomalies, and provide actionable insights without human intervention. Such systems will redefine industries by offering holistic solutions that combine sensory and linguistic intelligence, making AI a versatile collaborator in diverse settings.

2. From Responders to Autonomous Agents

Today's AI systems are reactive, producing outputs only when prompted. The next frontier is agentic AI, capable of initiating tasks, setting goals, and adapting strategies independently. These autonomous agents will maintain persistent context, allowing them to pursue long-term objectives without constant human oversight. Consider a legal research agent tasked with building a defense case: it could independently scour legal databases, draft arguments, and refine its analysis over time, all while adapting to new information. This shift will empower AI to function as a proactive partner, transforming workflows in professions like law, medicine, and project management. By reducing the need for micromanagement, autonomous agents will unlock new levels of efficiency and creativity, enabling humans to focus on strategic and innovative pursuits.

3. Blending Logic and Language: Neuro-symbolic AI

While current language models excel at generating fluent text, they often struggle with precise reasoning, leading to errors in logic or factual inaccuracies. Neuro-symbolic AI addresses this by combining the intuitive pattern recognition of neural networks with the structured logic of symbolic systems. This hybrid approach will enable AI to handle tasks requiring both creativity and precision. For example, in pharmaceutical research, a neural-symbolic AI could analyse scientific literature, extract key variables, and simulate chemical interactions with mathematical accuracy, then propose testable hypotheses. Such systems will thrive in domains like engineering, finance, and science, where rigorous reasoning is paramount. By bridging the gap between language and logic, Neuro-symbolic AI will deliver more reliable and insightful outcomes.

4. Memory and Identity: Persistent, Personalised AI

The transient nature of current AI interactions limits their ability to form meaningful, long-term relationships with users. Future systems will incorporate persistent memory, retaining conversational history, user preferences, and contextual nuances across sessions. This capability will allow AI to develop a sense of identity, tailoring its behaviour to individual needs. Imagine a lifelong educational AI that tracks a student's academic journey, adjusting its teaching methods based on their evolving strengths and weaknesses. Over years, it could foster intellectual growth by introducing concepts at the right pace and in the right context. This personalisation will make AI feel like a trusted companion, enhancing its role in education, healthcare, and personal development.

5. Personalisation and Privacy

As concerns about data privacy grow, centralised AI models that rely on cloud-based processing face scrutiny. Federated AI offers a solution by running smaller, specialised models on personal devices, ensuring data remains local while delivering tailored experiences. For instance, a fitness AI on a smartphone could analyse data from wearables and health apps to provide customised advice without transmitting sensitive information to external servers. This approach not only enhances privacy but also enables real-time responsiveness, as processing occurs on-device. Federated AI will democratise access to personalised technology, empowering users in areas like healthcare, finance, and lifestyle management while safeguarding their data.

6. Embodied AI: From Language to Action

Current AI is confined to digital environments, but the future lies in embodied AI, which integrates with robotics to interact with the physical world. These systems will combine sensory perception, reasoning, and physical action, enabling them to perform tasks in real-world settings. A warehouse robot, for example, could interpret verbal instructions, navigate complex environments, and manipulate objects with precision, all while providing status updates. This convergence of language and action will revolutionise industries like manufacturing, logistics, and healthcare, where AI-driven robots could assist with surgeries or eldercare. Embodied AI will bridge the gap between virtual intelligence and physical utility, creating systems that are as capable in the world as they are in conversation.

7. Specialised Intelligence: Modular and Efficient Models

The trend toward ever-larger language models is giving way to modular architectures, where smaller, domain-specific models collaborate to tackle complex tasks. These systems will be faster, more efficient, and highly accurate within their areas of expertise. In a hospital, for instance, separate AI modules might handle diagnostics, imaging analysis, and patient communication, coordinated by a central system to deliver comprehensive care. This modularity allows for scalability and customisation, as new modules can be added to address emerging needs. By prioritising efficiency over size, modular AI will make advanced intelligence accessible to smaller organisations and resource-constrained environments, broadening its impact across sectors.

8. Trust Through Transparency: Explainable AI

The opaque nature of current AI decision-making undermines trust, particularly in high-stakes fields like medicine or finance. Explainable AI will address this by providing clear, traceable rationales for its outputs, enabling users to understand and verify its reasoning. A financial planning AI, for example, could recommend investments and justify its choices with references to market trends, historical data, and user goals, allowing clients to follow its logic step-by-step. This transparency will be critical for regulatory compliance and user confidence, ensuring AI systems are accountable and reliable. As explainable AI becomes standard, it will foster greater adoption in sensitive domains, where trust is non-negotiable.

9. Modelling the Future: World Simulation and Dynamic Reasoning

To support strategic decision-making, future AI might build internal models of the world, simulating outcomes based on real-time data and probabilistic reasoning. These systems will anticipate consequences and evaluate scenarios, offering insights that extend beyond immediate queries. An urban planning AI, for instance, could model the long-term effects of infrastructure projects, predicting impacts on traffic, housing, and the environment. By integrating live data feeds and advanced analytics, it would enable policymakers to make informed choices with confidence. This capability will transform fields like governance, economics, and climate science, where understanding complex systems is essential for progress.

Are LLMs the answer to a futuristic world run totally by AI?

Well, the answer is No.

Despite the technological advancements, large language models (LLMs) have hit a significant bottleneck. What once seemed like limitless potential has started to level off as the performance gains from scaling up these models become less pronounced. While the earlier leaps in their capabilities were groundbreaking, the improvements seen in recent iterations have been marginal at best. The gap between the initial, rapid progress and the more recent, slower gains has become increasingly noticeable. As these models continue to grow in size and complexity, the results they yield become increasingly less impressive, highlighting the limitations of the current architecture.

The once-clear trajectory of progress that drove excitement in the field is no longer as visible, as each new version of these models brings diminishing returns in terms of performance. This slowdown in improvement serves as a reminder of the limits inherent in the current technological framework. Despite growing in size and sophistication, these models seem to be approaching a point where simply adding more data, processing power, and parameters does not necessarily lead to better results. The promise of limitless advancement has given way to a more tempered understanding of what is currently possible.

The core issue lies in the fact that LLMs, despite their remarkable ability to generate text and handle a wide array of queries, still struggle with more complex tasks. While they excel at producing text that is fluent and often convincing, these models face significant challenges when tasked with more intricate and demanding processes. Multi-step reasoning, maintaining coherence across long texts, and accurately interpreting nuanced instructions remain problematic. These are the areas where LLMs, despite their vast capabilities, fall short. Their responses often break down when faced with tasks that require a deeper understanding of context, or when the instruction involves multiple layers of reasoning.

As the size of these models continues to grow, the difficulty in navigating the complex webs of context that human communication involves becomes increasingly evident. The larger these models become, the harder it is for them to synthesise and manage the intricate relationships between different pieces of information, especially when that information spans long sections of text or requires holding onto context over extended periods. The models' capacity to process context is still limited, which often results in answers that are contextually relevant in isolated instances, but not when these threads are connected across a broader discussion.

While LLMs can produce text that appears logical on the surface, they still fail to grasp deeper meanings or respond to ambiguous prompts in a truly coherent manner. This lack of true understanding is most evident when the models are asked to make subtle inferences or respond to ambiguous situations. Their responses, though coherent in structure, frequently miss the underlying intent of the prompt, revealing that their "understanding" is still fundamentally superficial. They may excel at mimicking human-like language patterns, but they lack the deeper cognitive ability to fully comprehend the nuance or ambiguity that human communication inherently involves.

Alongside this, the computational demands for training and running these models have become increasingly unsustainable. As LLMs grow in size and complexity, the resources required to support their operation continue to escalate. The energy consumption associated with both the training process and the continuous running of these models has reached levels that are difficult to justify, given the returns.

The hardware needed to support these systems has grown more sophisticated and costly, with the requirements for high-end processors, vast memory capacities, and specialised infrastructure only increasing over time.

The financial costs involved in operating these models are similarly spiralling, placing a significant burden on organisations and institutions that continue to invest in their development. What was once a manageable investment is now becoming a substantial financial commitment, with costs rising in parallel with the demand for more powerful hardware and larger data centres. These growing expenses are increasingly difficult to sustain, especially when the returns from these investments in terms of performance improvements are becoming less significant.

This mounting burden makes the scaling of LLMs an inefficient path forward. The massive resources being poured into their development and operation no longer correspond to proportional gains in performance. As these models become larger and more complex, the diminishing returns on investment become ever more apparent, raising questions about the viability of simply scaling up further. The environmental impact, in addition to the increasing economic strain, creates further obstacles, limiting the practical scalability of such systems. The sheer scale of the energy consumption and hardware demands makes it difficult to envision these models expanding much further without significant changes in how they are developed and deployed.

The persistent problem of hallucination also remains a significant barrier. Despite ongoing efforts to refine and improve these models, LLMs continue to generate information that is inaccurate or entirely fabricated, with many users experiencing and reporting worse performance than before. While the tech companies continue to roll out improvements to the models, the quality of data plays an important role, especially when the internet is full of content that is not exactly considered good quality for LLMs to produce accurate information.

The downside of this is particularly felt in fields where precision is critical, such as healthcare, law, and scientific research, this unreliability undermines their usefulness and poses considerable risks. The consequences of relying on incorrect or fabricated information in these domains can be severe, ranging from misdiagnosis in healthcare to legal errors or flawed scientific conclusions. The stakes are high in these fields, and the inability of LLMs to guarantee the accuracy of their outputs makes their application in these contexts problematic at best, and potentially dangerous at worst.

As AI becomes more embedded in decision-making processes across various sectors, the importance of ensuring factual accuracy cannot be overstated. The integration of these systems into critical workflows demands a level of trust that, at present, LLMs have yet to consistently earn. The failure to resolve the issue of hallucination continues to be a major obstacle, and yet, LLMs still struggle with this fundamental problem. Despite the progress that has been made in refining these models, the core issue of generating accurate, verifiable information remains unresolved, limiting the scope of their practical application in areas where precision is paramount.

As these challenges persist, it becomes clear that the current trajectory of simply scaling up LLMs may no longer be enough. The relentless pursuit of larger models and more complex architectures has not yielded the breakthroughs many anticipated. While scaling has brought improvements, these advancements have started to plateau. It is becoming evident that simply increasing the size of these models is not the solution to the issues they face. To truly overcome these barriers, new approaches to model architecture, training methods, and data efficiency will be required. The focus needs to shift from merely expanding the scale to developing more efficient and innovative ways of training and refining these models.

Without these critical breakthroughs, LLMs may stagnate, unable to meet the growing expectations of both users and industries. The performance improvements seen in recent iterations have been incremental at best, leaving much to be desired. As industries and users continue to push for more sophisticated and reliable systems, the current limitations of LLMs may lead to frustration, and in turn, reduce confidence in their widespread adoption. The demand for AI that can deliver on its promises remains high, but the existing models, if left unchanged, may struggle to keep up.

While AI continues to integrate into daily life, the limitations of LLMs underscore the complexity of creating truly intelligent systems. These models have shown significant potential but also highlight how far we are from achieving artificial intelligence that can replicate the full range of human cognition and understanding. The gap between what LLMs can currently do and what is expected of them continues to widen, making it clear that we are still in the early stages of developing systems that can truly understand, reason, and act with the sophistication and depth of human intelligence.

Chart of Data Usage and CPU Power Over the Years

In recent years, AI has become the new buzzword, replacing machine learning and Business Intelligence (BI). The introduction of AlphaGo and its resounding victory over human players, including defeating the World Go champion, has sparked significant interest in AI-powered tools that are poised to chart the next trend for human society, ushering in a new era akin to the advent of the World Wide Web and the internet.

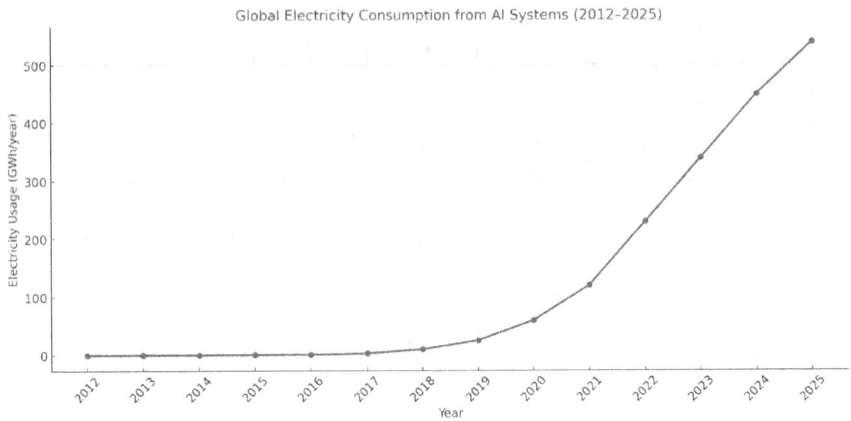

Artificial intelligence has evolved from a research-focused discipline to a cornerstone of global infrastructure. The sharp incline shown in the graph corresponds with key technological milestones and the mainstream adoption of AI across various industries. The values presented in the chart are not generic estimates of data centre consumption, nor do they account for peripheral technologies such as mobile networks or IoT infrastructure. Instead, this chart isolates the electricity required for training and deploying AI systems, with a particular focus on large language models (LLMs), image generators, recommendation engines, autonomous agents, and the inference engines running them at scale.

Time Period:

- **2012 to 2016**:
  In the early years of modern AI development, electricity usage remained relatively low. Research was primarily academic, confined to university clusters or modest-scale enterprise systems. The models developed during this period, including early versions of image recognition and basic natural language processing, required comparatively minimal computational power.

- **2017 to 2019**:
  This period marks the first significant rise in electricity demand, coinciding with the emergence of transformer-based architectures and the publication of models such as BERT (Google, 2018) and GPT-2 (OpenAI, 2019). These models required large GPU clusters for training, often necessitating multiple weeks of continuous computation on high-power hardware. Deployment began to expand from research labs into early commercial applications, including chatbots, auto-tagging systems, and predictive analytics.

- **2020 to 2022**:
  The line steepens dramatically. This phase saw the deployment of GPT-3, which contained 175 billion parameters and reportedly required approximately 1.3 GWh for training alone. Electricity usage soared as organisations began scaling inference systems for public use. AI transitioned into a cloud-native consumer product, embedded in tools ranging from writing assistants to customer service bots. The daily usage by millions of people introduced a constant baseline demand on the data centres running these models.

- **2023 to 2025 (projected)**:
  By this stage, electricity use has entered utility-scale proportions. LLMs like GPT-4, Claude, Gemini, and open-source equivalents were being deployed globally. Many are hosted on dedicated server farms drawing power in the megawatt range. What distinguishes this phase is not just the training costs, but the massive, always-on inference infrastructure. The amount of energy consumed by running these models continuously far exceeds the cost of training. Model size continues to increase, but the key multiplier has become usage volume: millions of users, billions of queries,

and expectations of sub-second response times have reshaped how electricity is consumed in digital infrastructures.

Note: These figures are rough estimates from the basic computational power for the data centres.

The current trajectory of electricity consumption driven by large language models is rapidly becoming unsustainable. Each new generation of models demands vastly more computational power, and with it, significantly more energy. Unlike earlier phases of AI development, where energy use scaled modestly, today's models exhibit exponential growth in resource demand. Training a single state-of-the-art LLM can consume as much electricity as hundreds of households do in a year, and that is before factoring in the cost of widespread daily use across millions of users. As shown in the chart, the energy curve is no longer a gentle incline but a sharp, accelerating climb. If this pattern continues, the environmental cost of running these models at scale will outweigh their utility, particularly in regions where power grids are already strained.

What impact can AI bring to human society?

The impact of Artificial Intelligence on human society is both profound and complex, with consequences that extend from immediate changes in the job market to broader, long-term shifts in how people relate to technology in daily life. One of the earliest and most visible effects is likely to be the replacement of particular segments of the workforce. As AI systems continue to evolve and are introduced across a growing number of industries, they are becoming more capable of handling tasks that have traditionally required human effort. In many cases, these systems can now perform such tasks not only with greater speed and accuracy, but also at a lower cost, making them an attractive alternative for businesses focused on efficiency.

For example, commission-based roles such as telemarketers, real estate agents, insurance brokers, and promoters are particularly vulnerable. In these fields, the nature of the job involves repetitive tasks that can be automated. From customer interactions, data gathering, lead generation, and follow-ups, these tasks are being replaced by workflow systems with machine learning capabilities to process the data into meaningful information. In the eyes of businesses, the efficiency of AI systems makes them an attractive alternative to human workers. Machines or systems that require less energy, cost, and maintenance can be seen as more profitable in the long run. If an AI system can perform tasks that previously required human intervention, such as managing calls, processing requests, or even negotiating deals, businesses are likely to adopt these systems to increase productivity, cut costs, and maximise profits. In the pursuit of efficiency and better returns, human workers may be viewed merely as components of a machine-like system, replaceable by more efficient alternatives when the right technology becomes available.

This shift raises important questions about the future of employment. Jobs in sectors like customer service, sales, marketing, and even administrative roles are at risk of being replaced by AI-driven processes. These sectors often rely on human communication and decision-making, but AI systems are increasingly able to replicate and even surpass these capabilities in some cases. This could lead to widespread job displacement, requiring societies to adapt by rethinking the future of work and redefining job roles for an AI-powered world.

In a conversation I had with a friend, we explored this very idea. He was considering a career change, looking to move from his mundane desk job in a bank to a more exciting career in property management. He had a genuine passion for real estate and had already invested in properties. However, he was fully aware that property management is no easy task. The job involves a multitude of responsibilities, from surveying properties and finding the right ones within budget to maintaining them and dealing with tenants. It is a complex and time-consuming process, especially when managing multiple properties at once.

He asked me for advice on setting up a system that would help him analyse data and streamline his operations. Initially, he only sought a tool to manage the day-to-day activities of property management, a common desire in many businesses undergoing digital transformation. He wanted a system that would make it easier to manage his properties and offer clients a platform to request additional services. But as we discussed further, it became clear that this was only a temporary solution. In the near future, AI will be capable of managing such operations entirely, providing solutions to problems before human intervention is needed.

Rather than relying on data scientists to sift through large datasets and use business intelligence tools to uncover insights, AI will already have the ability to interpret data and provide actionable recommendations. All we need to do is review the options it presents and make decisions based on that. This level of AI integration is inching us closer to a future that mirrors the sci-fi movies we have watched for years. Instead of manually entering commands or relying on voice assistants for basic tasks, our AI will proactively manage our schedules, workflows, and decision-making processes.

For instance, instead of having to say, "Hey Siri, please help me create a meeting with the vendor this afternoon," AI will already know the context of your day, your preferences, and the vendor's availability. It will be able to say something like, “Hi boss, based on your past activities and vendor requests, I have scheduled a meeting for you this afternoon. Does this time work for you, or would you like to choose a different time from these available options?”

This shift represents a monumental change in how we interact with technology. The AI assistant of the future will not simply respond to commands or requests, but will actively engage in the planning and decision-making process on our behalf. This evolution will transform the role of AI from a passive tool into an active participant in our daily routines. These systems will be capable of making suggestions based on a combination of data inputs, such as previous interactions, calendar events, personal preferences, and even real-time adjustments based on new data or changing circumstances. The AI assistant will become a true extension of ourselves, not only carrying out tasks but also anticipating our needs before they arise. It will offer us tailored options that will make our lives more efficient, allowing us to save time and effort in managing our day-to-day activities.

This is just one example of how AI is poised to transform daily life, not merely by automating repetitive tasks but by taking over entire processes, from decision-making to real-time adjustments. In the near future, we may find ourselves interacting with AI systems that can predict our needs before we even express them. These systems will have a level of foresight that will allow them to manage even the most complex aspects of our lives. From the simple act of scheduling meetings to more intricate tasks such as managing personal finances or planning long-term projects, AI will streamline every facet of daily life. Its ability to integrate with numerous data sources will make these processes not only more efficient but also more intuitive.

However, while this offers immense convenience, it also raises concerns about dependence on AI and the potential consequences of relinquishing so much control to algorithms. As we place more trust in AI to manage our personal lives, the risk of over-reliance becomes ever more real. We may begin to lose some of our ability to make decisions independently, relying too heavily on systems that, despite their intelligence, are still limited by the data they process. The more AI systems control, the more we risk losing our capacity to engage in decision-making without their intervention. This balance between convenience and autonomy will be a delicate one to strike.

Ultimately, as AI systems become more sophisticated, human society will need to adapt to this new reality. Some jobs will undoubtedly be lost as AI systems take over tasks traditionally performed by humans. Roles in sectors like manufacturing and administration may be significantly reduced, while other positions will emerge in fields like AI oversight, data ethics, and human-AI collaboration. New opportunities will arise in the development, maintenance, and regulation of AI, requiring a workforce skilled in navigating these complex systems. However, while technological progress creates new career paths, it also demands that society rethink its approach to employment and productivity.

Societies will need to rethink how to balance the convenience and efficiency AI offers with the need to preserve meaningful human employment and creativity. As AI systems take on more responsibilities, we will need to ensure that human workers can still find roles that allow them to contribute meaningfully to society. This will require both governmental and corporate intervention to retrain and support displaced workers while encouraging innovation that remains rooted in human creativity and emotional intelligence. The challenge will not just be technological but societal, as we must navigate the effects of AI on our cultures and economies.

This transformation is inevitable, but the challenge will lie in navigating this change in a way that benefits both individuals and the larger societal fabric. The choices we make today about how to implement AI and how to manage its integration into our lives will shape the future of human society. It will require thoughtful regulation, an understanding of the ethical implications, and a concerted effort to ensure that the benefits of AI are shared broadly, rather than concentrated in the hands of a few.

How can AI change the entire business ecosystem?

Once the technology is matured enough, AI can actually replace the role of a human manager. Managers, as we know from the title of the job itself, function by managing a group of staff, or multiple teams, to achieve the goals and objectives set by the owners of the company. Members of the team would often need to report their progress to their managers so that the progress could then be compiled and updated to the bosses by the managers. Managers would also review the health status of the projects, identify possible impediments or obstacles, and may suggest solutions for the owners to decide the next action. A manager would also monitor the performance of the staff under his or her supervision, and submit the annual staff appraisal, bonuses, or increments. Now, based on the job description, which of the tasks above cannot be accomplished by the AI? All the AI requires are data, data, and more data. AI as a manager will be more effective as an automated tool for the following:

1. Weekly reports or progress can be updated and presented instantly to the bosses without having to wait for the human managers to compile them into spreadsheets or presentation slides.
2. AI can provide suggestions or solutions to recurring problems immediately, or search through the internet for similar cases. The results will be available almost instantly.
3. No bias when it comes to giving out performance based on meritocracy.
4. Will never involve in office politics, means projects will go smoothly without all the dramas.
5. Unlike human managers, AI does not suffer from fatigue, emotional bias or personal conflicts, ensuring consistent and logical decision-making at all times.

6. AI can analyse vast amounts of employee performance data objectively, recommending promotions or salary adjustments purely based on data-driven results.
7. Project deadlines will be managed more effectively as AI can help to instantly evaluate workload distribution and adjust team allocations accordingly to maximise efficiency.
8. Communication breakdowns will be minimised, as AI can track all conversations, emails and progress logs to ensure no critical information is lost or misinterpreted.
9. Cost savings for companies will be significant, as an AI-driven management system does not require salaries, benefits or common trainings.
10. Businesses will operate with greater transparency, consistency and efficiency, completely transforming the traditional corporate hierarchy.

AI Usage Case Studies

Before the widespread use of LLMs for public usage, AI systems have been deployed by corporations to streamline operations, improve customer interactions, and foster innovation across sectors. Technologies like machine learning, computer vision, and predictive analytics enabled businesses to tackle complex challenges, from optimising logistics to automating services. These early AI efforts delivered measurable gains in efficiency and cost savings, shaping industries and laying the foundation for future advancements.

1. AI in Human Resource Management – Unilever

Unilever has adopted artificial intelligence in its recruitment process to streamline hiring and enhance decision-making. The company uses a platform called Pymetrics, which applies neuroscience-based games to evaluate candidates' cognitive and emotional traits. These assessments are designed to provide a more objective and standardised measure of potential, aiming to reduce the impact of unconscious bias in the early stages of candidate evaluation.

In the subsequent stages of recruitment, Unilever uses HireVue, an AI-driven video interview platform. Candidates record responses to preset questions, and the system analyses facial expressions, vocal tone, and language patterns to assess traits such as communication skills and emotional intelligence. The analysis is based on consistent criteria, offering a more data-driven approach to screening.

According to Unilever, the integration of these AI tools has reduced the time to hire by approximately 75 %. It has also contributed to greater diversity and inclusion by broadening the candidate pool and removing some traditional barriers in the hiring process. The company reports that the use of AI has improved overall candidate experience and allowed human recruiters to focus more on final-stage decision-making and cultural fit.

2. AI in Retail – Amazon

Amazon is a leader in applying artificial intelligence to transform the retail landscape. One of the most notable innovations is Amazon Go, a cashier-less retail store that uses AI to eliminate traditional checkouts. Shoppers scan their Amazon app on entry, take the items they want, and leave the store without stopping to pay. Behind the scenes, a combination of computer vision, sensor fusion, and deep learning tracks which products are taken from or returned to shelves. The system automatically charges the customer's Amazon account once they exit.

The Amazon Go system is supported by ceiling-mounted cameras, shelf sensors, and advanced tracking algorithms that identify both the shopper and the items in real time. The goal is to provide a seamless, frictionless shopping experience while reducing labour costs and increasing operational efficiency.

Beyond physical retail, Amazon's use of AI is deeply embedded in its recommendation engine, one of the core drivers of its e-commerce success. Machine learning models analyse a vast range of customer data, including past purchases, browsing behaviour, search history, reviews, and items in wish lists or shopping carts. This enables Amazon to deliver highly personalised product suggestions that adapt over time.

These AI-powered recommendations reportedly account for over 30 % of Amazon's total revenue. They also help improve user engagement, customer satisfaction, and conversion rates, making AI a cornerstone of Amazon's competitive advantage in online retail.

3. AI in Healthcare – IBM Watson Health

Artificial intelligence is playing a growing role in healthcare, and IBM Watson Health was one of the most high-profile early initiatives to apply AI to medical diagnostics and treatment support. Watson was developed to analyse large volumes of medical data, including patient records, clinical guidelines, peer-reviewed journals, and clinical trial outcomes. Its goal was to assist healthcare professionals in making faster, more informed decisions by surfacing relevant insights from complex data sets.

One of the key applications of Watson Health was in oncology, where it aimed to support oncologists in identifying personalised cancer treatment options based on a patient's genetic profile and clinical history. Notably, Memorial Sloan Kettering Cancer Center collaborated with IBM to train Watson on oncology-related content. The system was intended to recommend evidence-based treatment plans tailored to individual patients.

Hospitals and healthcare institutions across the world trialled Watson Health in areas such as cancer care, radiology, and clinical decision support. IBM promoted the platform as a way to improve diagnostic accuracy, reduce time to treatment, and ultimately lower healthcare costs by enabling earlier and more precise interventions.

However, while the initial promise was significant, IBM scaled back Watson Health in subsequent years after challenges in delivering consistent clinical value and widespread adoption. In 2022, IBM sold parts of Watson Health to an investment firm, and the brand no longer operates as an independent unit under IBM.

Despite this, the legacy of Watson Health demonstrates both the potential and limitations of early AI applications in healthcare. It highlighted the importance of reliable data, clinical validation, and seamless integration into medical workflows, lessons that continue to shape the development of newer AI systems in medicine today.

4. AI in Finance – JPMorgan's COiN

JPMorgan Chase has developed an AI platform called COiN (Contract Intelligence), which uses natural language processing (NLP) to analyse legal documents and financial contracts. COiN can rapidly process vast volumes of documentation, performing in seconds what previously required thousands of hours of manual review by legal and operations staff.

Initially, COiN was applied to review commercial loan agreements, where it extracts critical data points such as terms, clauses, and obligations. These documents are often long, complex, and filled with nuanced legal language. COiN uses machine learning and pattern recognition to interpret and classify this information with a high level of consistency and accuracy.

According to JPMorgan, COiN has allowed the bank to significantly reduce the time and cost associated with document review, while also improving accuracy and minimising human error. This AI-driven approach has streamlined internal processes, freed up legal and compliance teams for more strategic analysis, and enhanced the bank's operational efficiency.

The broader implication of COiN reflects a growing trend in the financial services sector, where AI tools are being used to handle high-volume, rule-based tasks that require precision. JPMorgan continues to invest in AI research and development, extending automation into areas such as fraud detection, customer service, and risk management.

5. AI in Manufacturing – A large manufacturing company

A large manufacturing company has integrated artificial intelligence into its industrial operations to optimise manufacturing and equipment performance. By combining Industrial Internet of Things (IIoT) technologies with AI-driven predictive maintenance, the company enables real-time monitoring of machinery across its factories and industrial assets.

Sensors embedded in equipment continuously collect data such as vibration, temperature, pressure, and usage patterns. AI models analyse this data to detect anomalies, forecast equipment wear, and predict failures before they happen. This approach allows for condition-based maintenance, reducing unplanned downtime and extending the lifespan of critical assets.

One of the platforms central to the company's digital industrial strategy was Predix, a cloud-based software platform developed to manage and analyse data from industrial machines. Using machine learning and analytics, Predix provided predictive insights that helped engineers schedule maintenance proactively, avoiding breakdowns and production interruptions.

The company reported that the use of predictive maintenance through platforms like Predix led to a reduction in unplanned downtime by up to 20% and a 25% decrease in maintenance costs. These improvements resulted not only in cost savings but also in increased safety and equipment reliability.

While the company has since scaled back the standalone commercial ambitions of the Predix platform, it continues to apply AI and IIoT within its industrial units, focusing on internal optimisation across aviation, power, and healthcare divisions.

6. AI in Marketing – A Large Beverage Company

A well-known beverage company employs artificial intelligence across multiple areas of its operations, particularly in marketing and supply chain optimisation. Through partnerships with companies like Google Cloud and Salesforce, The company integrates machine learning and AI into its digital strategies to improve customer engagement and operational efficiency.

In marketing, the beverage company uses AI-powered platforms, such as Salesforce Einstein, to analyse vast amounts of consumer data from social media, customer surveys, and loyalty programmes. This allows the company to develop personalised marketing campaigns based on customer preferences, increasing targeting precision and engagement. The company uses this data to optimise its advertisements, tailoring content that resonates with specific demographics.

The company also applies AI to improve its supply chain management. By collaborating with Microsoft Azure and SAP, the company uses AI to forecast demand, optimise inventory, and reduce waste. AI-driven demand prediction models incorporate data such as historical sales, seasonal trends, and external factors like weather events and calendar holidays, helping the company improve product availability across regions.

For logistics, the company uses AI-based route optimisation systems to streamline deliveries. These systems help plan the most efficient delivery schedules and routes, reducing fuel consumption and improving delivery speeds, which lowers operational costs and increases customer satisfaction.

These applications demonstrate the company's commitment to leveraging AI and data analytics across its business, enhancing its competitive advantage and operational effectiveness.

7. AI in Logistics – Logistic & Delivery Company

United Parcel Service (UPS) uses artificial intelligence to improve its logistics and delivery operations. Its On-Road Integrated Optimisation and Navigation (ORION) system optimises delivery routes for drivers. ORION analyses real-time data like traffic conditions, weather, delivery schedules, package priorities, and customer locations to generate the most efficient route for each driver. This minimises travel distance and time while maximising deliveries per trip.

ORION processes large datasets and considers up to 200,000 routing options per driver daily to provide tailored routes that adapt to changing conditions. It can reroute drivers to avoid sudden traffic delays or prioritise time-sensitive deliveries. This optimisation reduces fuel consumption. UPS reports savings of about 10 million gallons of fuel annually across its fleet. By shortening routes by an average of 6 to 8 miles per driver per day, ORION also lowers carbon emissions. This supports UPS's goal to achieve carbon neutrality by 2050.

UPS also uses AI-powered predictive analytics to forecast demand and streamline operations. Machine learning models analyse historical shipping data, seasonal trends, e-commerce patterns, and external factors like economic indicators to predict package volumes and delivery patterns. This helps UPS allocate resources efficiently. For example, it adjusts staffing levels, vehicle assignments, and sorting facility operations to handle peak periods like the holiday season. Predictive tools help UPS anticipate surges in specific regions to ensure adequate capacity without overextending resources.

UPS integrates AI into its logistics network through technologies like the Network Planning Tool (NPT). This complements ORION. NPT uses AI to optimise the broader supply chain and determine the most efficient paths for packages across sorting facilities, warehouses, and delivery hubs. By simulating scenarios and analysing variables like cost, speed, and capacity, NPT reduces transit times and operational costs. ORION and NPT together have helped UPS save hundreds of millions of dollars annually. ORION alone contributed to $400 million in savings by 2023, according to company reports.

UPS is also exploring AI-driven innovations to improve customer experience and operational resilience. Machine learning algorithms power chatbots and virtual assistants that handle customer inquiries, track packages, and resolve issues. This reduces call centre workloads. AI supports predictive maintenance for UPS's fleet of over 120,000 vehicles. It analyses sensor data to identify potential mechanical issues before they cause delays. This proactive approach minimises downtime and ensures reliable service.

By embedding AI across its operations, UPS has achieved measurable gains in efficiency, cost savings, and environmental impact. The company's investment in ORION, predictive analytics, and complementary tools shows how AI can transform logistics. It enables UPS to navigate the complexities of global delivery while meeting customer expectations and sustainability commitments.

8. AI in Autonomous Vehicles – Tesla

4Tesla leads the autonomous vehicle industry by integrating artificial intelligence into its self-driving technology. Its vehicles are equipped with AI systems that leverage computer vision, deep learning, and neural networks to process data from an array of sensors, including cameras, radar, and ultrasonic sensors. These systems enable Tesla cars to interpret their surroundings, navigate roads, detect obstacles, and make real-time driving decisions with minimal or no human input.

The cornerstone of Tesla's AI is its Autopilot system, which provides semi-autonomous driving capabilities. Autopilot uses a suite of eight cameras, twelve ultrasonic sensors, and forward-facing radar to create a 360-degree view of the vehicle's environment. The system's neural networks, trained on billions of miles of real-world driving data collected from Tesla's fleet, recognise objects like vehicles, pedestrians, and traffic signals. This allows features such as adaptive cruise control, lane-keeping, automatic lane changes, and self-parking. For example, Autopilot can maintain speed based on traffic conditions, steer within lanes, and execute manoeuvres like merging onto highways.

Tesla's Full Self-Driving (FSD) package builds on Autopilot, offering advanced features with the goal of achieving full autonomy. FSD enables capabilities like navigating city streets, responding to traffic lights and stop signs, and making turns at intersections. As of April 2025, FSD remains in a supervised beta phase, requiring driver oversight, but Tesla continues to refine it through over-the-air software updates. These updates improve performance by incorporating new data and refining neural network models, allowing vehicles to learn from diverse driving scenarios worldwide.

Tesla's AI development relies on its proprietary hardware and software ecosystem. The company's Hardware 4 (HW4) computer, deployed in newer models, processes sensor data at high speeds to support complex decision-making. Tesla's Dojo supercomputer accelerates neural network training by analysing vast datasets from its fleet, which has logged over 6 billion miles of FSD data by early 2025, according to company reports. This data-driven approach gives Tesla an edge in scaling its AI models compared to competitors reliant on smaller datasets or simulation-based training.

Beyond vehicle operation, Tesla uses AI to enhance safety and user experience. Predictive algorithms analyse sensor data to anticipate potential collisions, enabling automatic emergency braking or evasive manoeuvres. AI-powered features like Smart Summon allow vehicles to navigate parking lots and approach their owners autonomously. Tesla's in-car interface also employs AI to personalise driver settings and optimise navigation based on real-time traffic and user preferences.

9. AI in Customer Service – Zendesk

Zendesk leverages artificial intelligence to enhance customer service efficiency on its platform. The system uses chatbots, machine learning, and natural language processing to automate responses, resolve common inquiries, and escalate complex issues to human agents. By analysing millions of past interactions, the AI refines its answers over time, ensuring relevance and accuracy.

The Answer Bot is central to Zendesk's AI. It processes queries like billing issues or product questions, resolving about 40% of tickets without agent involvement, according to Zendesk's 2023 CX Trends Report. The bot scans a company's help articles to match customer intent, delivering instant answers. For unresolved cases, it routes tickets to agents with full context, like prior messages or account details, speeding up follow-ups. Machine learning also powers agent tools, suggesting replies based on successful resolutions. This cuts response times by 15-20%, per 2024 customer data.

Zendesk's AI excels for businesses handling high inquiry volumes. It reduces agent workload by up to 30% by automating repetitive tasks, freeing staff for nuanced cases, as reported in 2023 enterprise studies. Customer satisfaction rises about 10% due to faster, accurate responses, per Zendesk's 2023 CX Report. The system also predicts ticket surges using historical trends, helping managers staff teams proactively. For example, retailers prepare for holiday rushes without delays. By scaling support without quality loss, Zendesk's AI drives efficiency and loyalty, enabling companies to manage thousands of daily interactions while maintaining personalised service.

Are we ready for a full AI takeover?

With all the bells and whistles, the impressive feats displayed and achieved by ChatGPT, it still has its limitations, for now. The AI still lacks emotions that separate living with machines. Humans and animals have emotions and could express them with varying degrees of expression. We will grow attached to certain things around us, like the bond with our pets or even our possessions, AI and machines at this stage, can't. This emotional gap means AI struggles to understand or replicate the depth of human connections, like the loyalty a dog shows its owner or the nostalgia tied to a childhood toy. These bonds shape how we make decisions, from forgiving a friend to valuing a family heirloom, and AI cannot mimic that intuitive warmth.

There was an experiment conducted by the Japanese researchers to have the AI replace court judges so cases can be reviewed and decided much faster based on the evidence gathered. This experiment aimed to streamline Japan's legal system, where some trials drag on due to complex evidence or limited court resources. Punishments could be meted out decisively without the involvement of juries as they can be decided based on past cases. While it certainly can speed up the court procedures that would normally take years, clearing off all the backlog and reducing the workload of court officials, there is an argument if the AI did consider to reduce sentence due to his background and current circumstances, e.g. If the convict has shown regret and remorse over his crime, or he committed the crime out of desperation. The AI judge would certainly not feel any empathy with the convict. A person stealing a banana because he was hungry and a person stealing a purse to purchase drugs might be given similar prison sentences. Human judges often weigh factors like intent or hardship, such as a single parent stealing to feed kids, and adjust rulings accordingly, a nuance AI misses without explicit coding.

Therefore, even with the advancement of the AI algorithm and the many impressive feats that it can perform, there are still jobs that AI would not be able to replace. Professions such as therapists, psychologists, scientists, to name a few, will still have their place in our society in the future where AI and robotics would be running most of the jobs. Therapists listen and connect with clients' pain, while psychologists decode intricate emotions, tasks requiring a human touch AI can't fake. Scientists dream up hypotheses from curiosity, not just data, pushing boundaries in ways AI supports but doesn't lead. Personally, I would find AI hard to take over jobs that need to cater to the fussy and ever changing humans, like emotions, preferences, tastes. So maybe chefs are still able to keep their jobs, partially in the future, by focusing on experimenting with the new taste in order to satisfy the "always eager to try something new" masses. It might take tremendous effort for AI to put up with humans who might change their preference in the next second. Not convinced? Try getting an AI to deal with your girlfriend when trying to guess what she wants for dinner. I would bet the AI would crash before it is able to give an answer that would satisfy her. Jokes aside, the advancement of AI and its integration with our daily lives, it would spark a permanent change to our lives as we know it today. Chefs tweaking flavors for picky eaters or artists chasing trends show how human whims drive creativity, keeping these roles safe for now. In fact, the changes have started gradually until they are fully integrated in every aspect of our lives.

These are some of the scenarios where A.I will completely take over, for good or for the worse. AI already handles repetitive tasks like sorting data or scheduling, and it's set to dominate more, with studies suggesting 30% of routine jobs could be automated by 2030.

Full automation of the supply chain

AI can be deployed to fully automate the entire supply chain ecosystem. From setting up your company, procuring the goods to sell, establishing digital marketing strategy, making payment to your suppliers and receiving payment from customers, to sending accurate information to the tax agencies, everything can be automated and run on its own. Setting up your company gets faster with AI pulling industry data to pick the best structure, like retail or wholesale, without human guesswork. Payments to suppliers flow through instant digital transfers, and customer payments hit your account via automated checkout systems, all synced to keep money moving.

Through the use of data, AI could be used to automate the process of the mundane tasks like filling in the orders and sending them to the customers for replenishment. As your business grows, so will your data. AI can then utilise your sales data, along with your inventory to suggest the necessary procurements for stock replenishments. This will not only reduce excessive wastage especially if the staff procure the wrong stocks or buy too much stocks for the seasonal sales, it can also increase the efficiency of the procurement process where you are guaranteed to receive the goods before the start of the season. AI looks at last year's sales, spotting that hats sell big in fall, and orders them by August to beat the rush. It catches errors, like staff grabbing sandals for a snowy quarter, saving cash. Suppliers get the heads-up early, locking in stock before demand spikes, unlike slow manual orders that miss the mark.

Since data can be easily shared across, this allows all the parties involved to better prepare for any unforeseen circumstances with AI recognising the pattern for potential risk and generating the alert notification for action. If a shipment might stall due to a holiday backlog, AI pings everyone from warehouse to delivery crew to adjust timelines. It tracks risks, like a supplier's history of shorting orders, and sends warnings to switch sources, keeping the chain tight. This shared info means no one's caught off guard, smoothing out hiccups before they blow up.

From the customer data gathered thus far, AI can analyse customer behaviour and generate targeted advertisements to increase the likelihood of sales. Beyond that, AI can identify interests and patterns in recurring purchases, allowing it to categorise customers effectively. This segmentation enables the creation of personalised loyalty programmes, where different customers receive benefits most relevant to their habits. As a result, customer retention rates increase significantly compared to companies that do not leverage customer data in their loyalty strategies. For example, AI can detect customers who purchase socks monthly and target them with ads for new styles, offering special pricing to encourage further purchases. It can also assign perks such as free returns to frequent buyers, while occasional shoppers receive timely discount codes to maintain engagement. This approach outperforms generic loyalty schemes by eliminating wasted effort on one-size-fits-all rewards, with studies in 2024 showing double-digit improvements in retention.

Marketing becomes more precise with AI, timing advertisements to match customer shopping habits. For example, it targets late-night online browsers when interest is highest. It identifies trending products from sales data and promotes them in real time, riding demand instead of relying on outdated, static strategies. Procurement stays lean as AI monitors inventory daily, ordering just enough to meet demand and avoiding excess stock. Payments to suppliers are processed quickly, with AI matching invoices to purchase orders automatically. On the customer side, payment links speed up transactions and reduce delays. Even tax reporting benefits, with clean data on sales and supplier costs submitted on time, helping companies avoid the penalties that hit less organised firms.

As your business scales, AI processes larger datasets to keep procurement accurate, ordering for new regions without relying on guesswork. It accelerates supplier payments by batching them weekly, while customer payments arrive through more channels, such as mobile apps, without requiring additional staff. Risk alerts become more intelligent, identifying patterns like seasonal shipping disruptions and notifying teams to adjust, ensuring goods continue to move efficiently. Customer advertising becomes even more refined, targeting niche behaviours such as late-night snack buyers to lift sales. At the same time, loyalty perks adapt to keep each customer segment engaged, helping to strengthen your competitive advantage.

Resource Optimisation for Logistics

AI transforms resource optimisation in logistics by streamlining operations and reducing waste. It manages fleet efficiency, ensuring trucks run full and on shortest routes, cutting fuel use. For example, The AI system analyses traffic patterns, delivery schedules, and load capacities to group shipments, avoiding half-empty trips. In 2024, logistics firms using AI routing saved 12% on fuel costs, per industry data. This precision also lowers wear on vehicles, extending their lifespan and slashing maintenance expenses.

Warehouse management benefits too. AI systems are used to track inventory in real time, matching stock levels to demand so goods move out fast, not sitting unused. It predicts peak periods, like holiday rushes, and shifts resources, such as extra forklifts or staff hours, to handle the surge without overcommitting. This cuts storage costs and spoilage, especially for perishables like fruit, where AI priorities shipping based on expiration dates. Companies adopting AI warehouse tools reduced waste by 18% in 2023, according to supply chain reports.

AI systems are also used to optimise human resources. It schedules drivers and warehouse crews based on workload, avoiding idle time or overtime. By forecasting delays, like road closures, AI adjusts shifts early, keeping teams productive. This balances labor costs with output, ensuring no one's paid to stand around. In 2024, AI-driven scheduling trimmed labor expenses by 10% for major carriers, per logistics studies.

Risk management ties it together. AI spots bottlenecks, like a dock overloaded with incoming trucks, and reroutes or re-schedules to keep flow smooth. It flags fuel price spikes, suggesting bulk buys or route tweaks to offset costs. This proactive stance maximises every resource, from gas to time, making logistics leaner and more responsive than manual methods ever could.

Medical Condition Alerts Through Monitoring

Artificial intelligence's role in medical monitoring hinges on its ability to process vast streams of physiological data in real time, transforming raw inputs from sensors, wearables and implants into actionable insights. At the core of these systems are machine learning models trained to detect anomalies that evade human perception. For example, photoplethysmography (PPG) sensors in devices such as the Apple Watch or Fitbit capture pulse waveforms by measuring blood flow changes under the skin. These waveforms are fed into convolutional neural networks (CNNs), which analyse micro-variations in rhythm and amplitude to flag arrhythmias such as atrial fibrillation (AFib). Unlike traditional threshold-based alarms, which trigger alerts for fixed parameters (for example, heart rate exceeding 120 BPM), AI contextualises data. It distinguishes between benign spikes (such as during exercise) and pathological patterns (such as ventricular tachycardia), reducing false alarms by up to 60% in ICU settings. PPG data, collected every few seconds, gives CNNs millions of data points daily, letting them spot subtle shifts, like irregular beats missed by overworked staff. In busy ICUs, where nurses juggle multiple patients, this cuts noise from constant beeping, letting teams focus on real emergencies. Studies from 2023 show AI catching AFib up to 30 minutes before doctors, saving critical time.

Federated learning (FL) has emerged as a pivotal approach in healthcare AI, enabling multiple institutions to collaboratively train models without sharing sensitive patient data. This method has been particularly beneficial in critical care settings, such as intensive care units (ICUs), where timely interventions are crucial.

For instance, an adaptive FL framework was proposed to address data distribution drift across different institutions. This framework separated input features into stable, domain-specific, and conditional-irrelevant parts according to their relationships to clinical outcomes. Evaluations on tasks like predicting the onset risk of sepsis and acute kidney injury (AKI) demonstrated that this approach outperformed existing FL baselines and provided clinically interpretable results.
Another study, FLICU, introduced a federated learning workflow for ICU mortality prediction. By extracting multivariate time series data from the MIMIC-III database, the study benchmarked the predictive performance of various deep sequential classifiers. The results indicated that federated learning could serve as a valid and privacy-preserving alternative to centralised machine learning for classifying ICU mortality when sharing sensitive patient data between hospitals is not feasible.

Additionally, the FedSepsis project demonstrated the feasibility of implementing federated learning on low-end computational devices like Raspberry Pi and Jetson Nano. By utilising multimodal data from electronic health records, the system achieved high accuracy in early sepsis detection, with an average earliness of 4.56 hours.

These examples underscore the potential of federated learning in enhancing clinical decision-making while safeguarding patient privacy. However, challenges such as data heterogeneity, model convergence, and the need for robust validation remain. Ongoing research and collaboration are essential to address these issues and fully realise the benefits of federated learning in healthcare AI.

AI also refines monitoring with wearables tracking sleep or stress. Fitbit's PPG sensors log heart rate variability (HRV), feeding CNNs to detect stress patterns, like HRV dipping during chronic anxiety, alerting users to rest. In implants, like cardiac pacemakers, AI scans electrical signals for failures, notifying doctors if pacing falters, cutting response time from days to hours. Federated learning extends to rare conditions, pooling data from global clinics on diseases like pulmonary hypertension, spotting signs like oxygen dips paired with fatigue, all while keeping patient IDs locked. Edge AI in ICU ventilators adjusts oxygen flow by analysing breathing rates, catching distress like shallow gasps, and tweaking support instantly, unlike slower manual checks.

This scales monitoring beyond hospitals. Wearables sync with phone apps, letting AI warn of fever trends in flu season, nudging users to test early. Glucose predictions from edge devices like Dexcom pair with food logs, suggesting carb intake to steady levels, empowering patients daily. Federated models grow smarter as more hospitals join, refining anomaly detection, like sepsis flags from subtle vitals shifts, without privacy risks. By processing data where it's born, AI keeps care fast and sharp, turning raw numbers into life-saving calls with precision humans alone can't match.

Case Studies

1. Predicting Cardiac Arrest in Post-Surgical Patients

In 2022, John Hopkins Hospital deployed an AI system across its ICU and general units to address the high mortality rate of postoperative sepsis. The system integrated data from bedside monitors (heart rate, oxygen saturation), lab results (white blood cell counts, lactate) and even nurse notes (free-text entries about patient demeanour). Using long short-term memory (LSTM) networks, the AI detected subtle correlations, such as a 0.5°C temperature rise paired with a 10% increase in respiratory rate, which human clinicians often overlooked. Over six months, the algorithm flagged sepsis risk in hundreds of patients hours earlier than standard protocols. Mortality rates dropped by 18%, and hospital stays shortened by three days, saving a substantial amount of money in care costs.

Critically, the system's success relied on federated learning. By training on anonymised data from dozens of hospitals without centralising records, it avoided privacy breaches while achieving around 89% accuracy. However, challenges emerged. In one instance, the AI misclassified a patient's post-surgical inflammation as sepsis, leading to unnecessary antibiotics. This underscored the need for hybrid systems where AI suggestions are validated by clinicians.

2. Mental Health Relapse Detection via Voice Analysis

An AI startup spun out of MIT, developed a mental health monitoring tool that analyses vocal biomarkers during routine phone calls. The system uses natural language processing (NLP) to track speech patterns, such as a slowing cadence, prolonged pauses or monotone delivery, which correlate with depression relapses. In a 2022 trial with the US Department of Veterans Affairs, the AI monitored 1,200 veterans during weekly check-in calls. It flagged close to 85% of relapses two weeks before clinical assessments, enabling early interventions such as adjusted medication or therapy sessions.

The technology hinges on acoustic models trained on thousands of hours of speech from patients with diagnosed depression, PTSD and bipolar disorder. By isolating features such as jitter (microfluctuations in pitch) and shimmer (amplitude variations), the AI quantifies emotional flatness or agitation. However, ethical concerns arose when insurers began accessing these data to adjust premiums. In 2023, a class-action lawsuit alleged that UnitedHealth raised rates for veterans flagged as *high-risk* by AI, sparking debates about data ownership and algorithmic transparency.

3. Epilepsy Seizure Alerts in Ambulatory Settings

Epilepsy management has a long history of relying on in-hospital electroencephalogram (EEG) monitoring, which is costly and impractical for daily life. The Embrace2 wristband, developed by Empatica, disrupts this paradigm. Equipped with accelerometers and electrodermal activity sensors, it detects convulsive seizures by analysing arm movements and sweat gland activation. The AI model, trained on data from 1,800 epilepsy patients, distinguishes seizures from mundane activities (for example, chopping vegetables) with 94% accuracy.

In a phase 3 multi-centre prospective study published in the *Canadian Journal of Neurological Sciences*, 152 individuals aged six years and older participated in a continuous evaluation of the Embrace2 device across multiple epilepsy monitoring units. The study found a 94.0% sensitivity in detecting generalised tonic-clonic seizures (GTCS) with a 0.57 false alarm rate per 24 hours. The average detection latency was 37.46 seconds during rest periods, and no false alarms were reported during these periods (Kanner et al., 2021).

Ethical and Technical Challenges

While AI-driven monitoring saves lives, it risks amplifying healthcare inequities. Pulse oximeters and AI trained predominantly on light-skinned patients misread oxygen levels in darker-skinned individuals, as revealed in a 2022 *New England Journal of Medicine* study. This bias delayed critical care for Black and Hispanic patients, increasing mortality rates by 34% in severe COVID-19 cases. Similarly, glucose monitors such as the Dexcom G7 perform poorly on patients with lipodystrophy, a condition common in HIV survivors, due to training data gaps.

Another issue is alert fatigue. Nurses in ICUs equipped with AI systems report ignoring up to 40% of alerts due to sheer volume, per a 2023 survey. At one of the hospitals, a nurse dismissed an AI sepsis warning for a recovering appendectomy patient, assuming it was another false alarm. The patient later developed septic shock, surviving only after emergency surgery. Hybrid workflows, where AI prioritises alerts and humans validate them, are now seen as the gold standard.

Driverless vehicles

Autonomous vehicles rely on artificial intelligence to interpret sensor data, navigate dynamic environments and make real-time decisions. The core technology integrates lidar (light detection and ranging), radar (radio detection and ranging) and computer vision systems to create a 360-degree perception of the vehicle's surroundings. Machine learning models, such as convolutional neural networks (CNNs), process visual inputs from cameras to identify pedestrians, traffic signals and road markings. Simultaneously, reinforcement learning algorithms simulate millions of driving scenarios to train systems in avoiding collisions and optimising routes. The CNNs take camera data to spot a pedestrian stepping off a curb or a traffic signal turning red, critical for safe navigation. Reinforcement learning uses those millions of scenarios to teach the system how to dodge a sudden obstacle or pick a quicker route around traffic, all based on simulated practice.

Sensor fusion is critical. Lidar provides high-resolution 3D maps of the environment, radar detects the speed and distance of objects in poor weather, and cameras capture contextual details such as traffic light colours. These data streams are combined using Kalman filters to reduce noise and improve accuracy. For instance, Waymo's fifth-generation autonomous system employs a custom lidar sensor with a 300-metre range, paired with radar that operates effectively in rain and fog. The AI then uses behavioural cloning to mimic human driving patterns, such as yielding to merging traffic or navigating roundabouts. Lidar's 3D maps show the shape of a car ahead or a tree on the side, while radar measures how fast that car moves even in heavy rain. Cameras pick up the green of a traffic light, and Kalman filters blend all this to keep the AI's view sharp, cutting through weather haze. Waymo's system uses its 300-metre lidar to see far-off objects like a truck merging, with radar tracking its speed in fog, and behavioural cloning ensures the vehicle yields smoothly or circles a roundabout like a human would.

The AI interprets sensor data by pulling lidar's detailed maps, radar's motion readings, and camera visuals together for a full picture around the vehicle. CNNs process those visual inputs to catch road markings like a lane line or a stop bar, vital in busy streets. Reinforcement learning runs millions of driving scenarios, training the system to avoid a crash with a swerving bike or optimise a route past a jam. Lidar's high-resolution 3D maps outline the environment, from curbs to signs, while radar spots the distance and speed of a bus in drizzle. Cameras grab traffic light colours, like yellow turning red, and Kalman filters tie it all into one accurate feed for the AI to act on.

Case Studies

1. Urban Navigation in Complex Environments

In 2023, a tech company deployed its driverless taxis across downtown San Francisco, a city notorious for steep hills, dense fog and erratic pedestrian behaviour. The vehicles used a combination of lidar, radar and thermal cameras to detect cyclists swerving between lanes and jaywalkers obscured by fog. During a six-month trial, the AI successfully navigated 98% of trips without human intervention, reducing traffic violations by 40% compared to human drivers.

However, the system struggled with construction zones where temporary signage conflicted with pre-mapped data, requiring engineers to implement real-time semantic segmentation algorithms that distinguish permanent infrastructure from temporary obstructions. Lidar mapped the contours of steep hills, spotting a cyclist weaving through traffic at 20 kph, while radar tracked their distance in fog cutting visibility to 10 metres. Thermal cameras picked up the heat signature of a jaywalker darting across a street, invisible to standard lenses in San Francisco's mist.

The taxis' sensors worked together to handle the city's chaotic streets, where pedestrians often ignored crosswalks. Lidar built 3D models of intersections, catching a biker splitting lanes on a 15% incline, while radar gauged their speed despite drizzle. Thermal cameras flagged a pedestrian stepping out from behind a parked van, their body heat clear against the cold pavement, letting the AI brake in time. The 98% success rate came from navigating these scenarios, like climbing Lombard Street's curves or dodging walkers at Market Street, without needing a human to take over. The 40% drop in violations meant fewer lane drifts or missed stops compared to human cabbies, who often misjudged fog or hills.

Construction zones threw curveballs, with orange cones and new signs popping up overnight. The AI's pre-mapped data expected fixed lanes, but temporary barriers at sites like Van Ness Avenue confused it, risking stalls or wrong turns. Engineers rolled out semantic segmentation to parse camera feeds, labelling a concrete divider as permanent but a plywood board as temporary, so the AI could adjust its path. These algorithms ran in real time, processing lidar scans and camera images to spot a detour sign blocking a lane, keeping the taxi on course despite unmapped changes.

The trial covered thousands of trips, with sensors feeding the AI constant data to tackle San Francisco's quirks. Lidar outlined the city's jagged terrain, radar measured a scooter's approach through fog, and thermal cameras caught pedestrians blending into crowds, ensuring the AI stayed alert. The 98% autonomous rate held across busy spots like Union Square, where walkers surged unpredictably, and the violation reduction showed in cleaner stops at lights versus human drivers' slips. Semantic segmentation grew critical at construction-heavy zones, like near the Transbay Terminal, where the AI learned to ignore a taped-off sidewalk but was aware of a new stop sign, blending sensor inputs to make split-second calls.

2. Freight Logistics in Remote Areas

In Australia's Pilbara region, Rio Tinto has implemented autonomous haul trucks equipped with Autonomous Haulage System (AHS) technology to transport iron ore across extensive desert terrains. These trucks utilize predefined GPS courses to navigate haul roads and intersections, ensuring precise location tracking and coordination with other vehicles.

Since initiating trial operations in 2008, Rio Tinto's autonomous fleet has moved over one billion tonnes of ore and waste material across five sites in the Pilbara, including the Silvergrass mine. The autonomous trucks have operated approximately 700 hours more than conventional haul trucks annually, resulting in a 15% reduction in load and haul unit costs. Importantly, there have been zero injuries attributed to autonomous haul trucks since their deployment, highlighting their significant safety advantages.

In 2024, Rio Tinto collaborated with BHP, Caterpillar, and Komatsu to trial battery-electric haul trucks in the Pilbara, aiming to achieve net-zero operational greenhouse gas emissions by 2050.

3. Ethical Decision-Making in Critical Scenarios

Autonomous driving systems in 2024 began adopting frameworks to address the ethics of unavoidable road accidents. Their AI is programmed to prioritise the safety of vehicle occupants in critical situations, for instance, when swerving to avoid a pedestrian might cause a collision with a roadside barrier. This decision-making approach, driven by algorithms assessing moral utility, has provoked significant controversy. Critics argue it unfairly favours those inside the vehicle, often wealthier individuals who can afford such advanced technology, over vulnerable road users like pedestrians or cyclists, raising urgent questions about fairness in automated systems.

To counter the criticism, developers of these systems have released transparency reports to clarify how their technology functions. These reports outline how AI evaluates key factors, such as the speed of a potential collision, the condition of the road surface, and whether children are present nearby. By sharing such details, the industry seeks to address public concerns, aiming to show that autonomous vehicles strive to balance safety with ethical considerations in complex, life-or-death scenarios.

Ethical and Technical Challenges

Autonomous vehicles confront significant challenges in achieving universal adoption, critical for their integration into modern transport systems. Sensor technology remains a persistent limitation, particularly in adverse weather and lighting. For instance, lidar struggles with heavy snowfall, which scatters laser beams and reduces detection range by approximately 50%, while cameras are often blinded by direct sunlight, cutting obstacle recognition by up to 30%. Such vulnerabilities have led to incidents where vision-based systems failed to detect objects in bright conditions, contributing to collisions that underscore the need for robust solutions. Regulatory fragmentation further complicates deployment. The European Union mandates ISO 21434 cybersecurity standards, ensuring all new vehicles since 2024 are fully compliant with digital security requirements. In contrast, the United States lacks federal regulations, with 26 states establishing their own autonomous vehicle testing rules by 2023, resulting in varied safety protocols that hinder consistent progress.

Public trust poses another formidable barrier to widespread acceptance. Surveys indicate significant apprehension, with around 55% of UK drivers expressing distrust in autonomous vehicles due to fears of software glitches or cyberattacks that could jeopardise safety. To address these concerns, the industry has launched extensive public education campaigns, engaging approximately 500,000 people by 2024 through simulated rides and transparent incident reports that highlight safety performance, such as low collision rates. These initiatives aim to build confidence, demonstrating the reliability of autonomous systems and fostering their gradual integration into everyday life.

Resource Optimisation

Artificial intelligence significantly enhances resource optimisation by analysing intricate datasets to forecast demand, streamline operations, and reduce waste across sectors such as energy, logistics, and manufacturing. At its core, AI leverages predictive analytics to anticipate consumption trends, reinforcement learning to model potential decision outcomes, and digital twin technology to construct virtual replicas of physical systems, enabling precise real-time adjustments. In energy grids, for instance, AI systems process historical consumption data, weather predictions, and renewable energy capacities to dynamically balance supply and demand, achieving up to 20% reductions in outages. Machine learning algorithms, such as gradient boosting machines, forecast peak load periods with 95% accuracy, allowing utilities to allocate resources efficiently, prevent blackouts, and optimise grid performance.

In manufacturing, AI-driven predictive maintenance monitors equipment conditions, including vibrations, temperatures, and acoustic signals, to identify anomalies before they lead to costly failures. These systems employ auto-encoders, a form of neural network, to establish normal operational patterns and detect deviations, achieving fault detection rates of up to 90%. Similarly, in agriculture, AI utilises satellite imagery and soil moisture sensors to refine irrigation schedules, significantly reducing water usage while preserving crop yields. Such precision agriculture techniques, applied globally, enhance sustainability by ensuring resources are used judiciously, supporting industries in meeting efficiency and environmental goals.

Case Studies

1. Energy Grid Management

In regions where wind power accounts for a substantial portion of electricity generation, often exceeding 50%, artificial intelligence supports the management of complex energy grids reliant on renewable sources. Between 2022 and 2023, wind energy contributed approximately 50-55% to total electricity output in some areas, requiring precise forecasting to balance supply with fluctuating demand. AI models process extensive datasets, including historical consumption records, real-time weather patterns, and renewable energy capacities, to predict wind generation up to 36 hours in advance. These predictions achieve accuracy rates of 90-95%, enabling grid operators to anticipate production peaks and troughs with confidence. The integration of such data involves analysing variables like wind speed, temperature, and consumer usage trends, which vary significantly across seasons and times of day.

A key focus of these AI systems is minimising curtailment, the loss of surplus wind energy when generation outstrips immediate needs. In 2023, grid operators used AI to adjust energy flows, achieving efficiency improvements of around 20% by redirecting excess power to alternative uses. During periods of extreme weather, such as high-wind storms, AI algorithms reroute surplus energy to storage facilities, including those for hydrogen production, to prevent overloading the grid infrastructure. These systems continuously monitor demand spikes, particularly during peak hours, and allocate resources to maintain stability. By processing real-time inputs, AI ensures that energy distribution aligns closely with consumption patterns, reducing the frequency of disruptions and optimising the use of renewable resources across interconnected grid networks.

2. Retail Inventory Optimisation

Large retail chains, operating thousands of stores across diverse markets, employ artificial intelligence to manage inventory levels and reduce inefficiencies. AI algorithms analyse a wide range of data, including purchasing patterns, seasonal fluctuations, and local events like major hurricanes, to forecast product demand with high accuracy. During severe storms, these systems detect significant demand surges for essential items, such as bottled water and batteries, with increases ranging from 200-400% in affected regions. By processing data on consumer behavior, weather forecasts, and regional logistics, AI triggers automated restocking orders to warehouses, ensuring that stores remain supplied during critical periods. This process involves evaluating sales histories, delivery schedules, and even traffic patterns to optimise distribution.

In 2023, AI-driven inventory management reduced stockouts by 20-35%, ensuring customers could access needed goods, while also cutting perishable food waste by 10-20% through better alignment of stock with demand. Initial challenges arose when algorithms overestimated demand for non-essential products, leading to excess inventory costing millions. To address this, developers integrated sentiment analysis of social media trends, capturing real-time shifts in consumer preferences, such as reactions to local festivals or unexpected disruptions. This refinement required training models on diverse datasets, including online posts and regional demographics, to improve prediction accuracy. The systems now adjust forecasts daily, factoring in variables like promotional campaigns and supply chain constraints, to maintain balanced inventories across extensive retail networks, ensuring resources are allocated efficiently in response to dynamic market conditions.

3. Water Conservation in Sub-Saharan Africa

In drought-prone regions of Sub-Saharan Africa, AI platforms support agriculture by addressing water scarcity and processing data that enhance crop resilience. These systems combine satellite imagery, soil moisture sensors, and climate models to forecast drought risks several months in advance, achieving prediction accuracies of around 85%. In 2022, thousands of smallholder farmers received AI-driven guidance to switch from water-intensive crops to drought-resistant varieties, such as sorghum, which thrives in low-rainfall conditions. By analysing soil conditions, rainfall patterns, and crop suitability, AI recommended planting schedules that aligned with local climates, resulting in yield increases of 20-30% despite substantially reduced rainfall. The process involved mapping farmland remotely and cross-referencing data with weather forecasts to prioritise hardy crops.

AI also streamlines irrigation by processing real-time data on crop growth stages and evapotranspiration rates, determining precise water needs for each field. These systems integrate sensor readings from farms, capturing moisture levels hourly, and adjust irrigation schedules to minimise waste. In 2022, such optimisations led to substantial water savings, with studies indicating reductions of 20-40% in agricultural water use across similar initiatives. Farmers accessed recommendations via mobile platforms, receiving alerts on optimal planting and watering times based on local conditions. By tailoring resource use to environmental constraints, AI supported the cultivation of sustainable crops, enabling communities to maintain food production in the face of prolonged dry spells and variable weather patterns, with ongoing data analysis ensuring adaptability to changing agricultural needs.

Ethical and Technical Challenges

While AI-driven resource optimisation offers significant benefits, it raises ethical concerns about environmental trade-offs. Training large AI models, such as those used by Google DeepMind, consumes vast amounts of energy. These models, critical for tasks like forecasting energy demands or streamlining logistics, require thousands of processors running for weeks, drawing 100-1,000 megawatt-hours from data centres. A 2019 study by the University of Massachusetts found that training a single transformer model emits approximately 300 tonnes of CO2, equivalent to about 60 cars driven for a year. Cooling systems, needed to manage server heat, consume up to 40% of a centre's electricity, often from fossil-heavy grids. Once deployed, these models reduce carbon footprints by optimising energy grids, cutting emissions by 10-20% through analysis of consumption patterns, weather forecasts, and renewable outputs. Industries schedule training during renewable energy peaks, processing datasets on usage trends to lessen impacts, as computational needs grow with larger models. This creates a paradox where systems designed to reduce carbon footprints contribute to climate change, as training demands escalate alongside operational benefits.

Another issue is labour displacement. In logistics, autonomous AI systems at companies such as Amazon have reduced reliance on human workers for warehouse management and delivery routing. These systems deploy robots to sort packages, handling 70% of tasks in large warehouses, scanning thousands of items daily. Algorithms calculate routes using traffic data, fuel costs, and delivery schedules, adapting to peaks like holiday seasons. A 2017 International Labour Organisation report estimated that 14-20 million jobs in manufacturing and logistics could be automated by 2030, disproportionately affecting low-skilled workers in developing nations, where 60% of automation impacts occur. Retraining programs, teaching skills like system oversight, enroll thousands yearly but face funding shortages, leaving workers to adapt to mechanized tasks like picking or driving. Firms update AI with metrics on delivery speeds, ensuring efficiency, as automation expands across supply chains, reshaping workforce needs.

Data bias also undermines optimisation efforts. Recently, a European supermarket chain's AI system allocated fewer delivery trucks to underserved areas after training on historical sales data that reflected reduced spending power. These datasets, covering years of purchases, led algorithms, affecting 15% of retail AI systems, to prioritize high-revenue zones, limiting access to goods like fresh produce. This perpetuated challenges in community supply, prompting regulators to mandate fairness audits for AI resource allocation tools by 2024, with 20% of reviews targeting biases. Audits examine sales trends and demographics, requiring retailers to adjust models monthly with data on population or events. Compliance teams monitor thousands of predictions, ensuring deliveries meet needs, as systems refine allocations to balance efficiency with access.

Agri Tech to Boost Harvest Yields

Artificial intelligence in agriculture leverages sensor networks, satellite imagery, and machine learning models to optimise crop management, pest control, and resource allocation. Sensor networks, buried in fields, measure soil moisture, temperature, and nutrient levels every few hours, transmitting data to cloud platforms for analysis. Satellite imagery scans crops daily, capturing growth patterns across thousands of hectares to identify stress or pest damage. Machine learning models process these inputs, detecting anomalies, with adoption in precision farming reaching 80%.

Key technologies include hyper-spectral imaging, which captures light reflectance across hundreds of wavelengths to detect nutrient deficiencies. This technique measures plant chlorophyll and nitrogen levels, pinpointing areas needing fertiliser with 95% accuracy. Predictive analytics forecasts weather patterns and disease outbreaks by analysing decades of rainfall, temperature, and pest data. These systems warn farmers of risks such as blight or drought, achieving 85 to 90% accuracy.

For instance, AI systems analyse soil moisture, pH levels, and historical yield data to generate planting maps that guide farmers on optimal seed density and fertiliser application. These maps tailor planting to soil variations, boosting yields by 15 to 25% across crops like maize and wheat. Reinforcement learning algorithms further refine irrigation schedules by balancing water usage with predicted rainfall, reducing waste by 20 to 40%. These algorithms adjust water pumps daily, factoring in humidity, crop growth stages, and forecasts to ensure fields receive precise hydration based on real-time environmental shifts.

Autonomous machinery, such as AI-driven tractors and harvesters, uses computer vision to navigate fields while avoiding crop damage. These machines analyse live video feeds, recognising plants with 90% accuracy to steer through rows, cutting losses by 10 to 15%. They integrate real-time data from drones and ground sensors to adjust planting depth, herbicide spraying, and harvesting timing. Drones, flying hourly, map weeds or dry spots across fields, while ground sensors track soil compaction and moisture. By 2024, 70% of systems use such data for efficiency gains of around 20%. Tractors set seed depths by soil type to ensure germination, while sprayers target weeds with millimetre precision, reducing chemical runoff. Harvesters adapt blade heights for crops like barley, maximising output.

In livestock farming, AI monitors animal health through wearable collars that track body temperature, movement patterns, and feeding behaviour, enabling early disease detection. These collars log data every minute, identifying fever or reduced feeding with 85% accuracy and reducing mortality by 10 to 20%. Farmers receive alerts on mobile devices, allowing them to adjust diets or contact veterinarians as systems process herd trends and manage cattle or sheep across grazing cycles.

Case Studies

1. Precision Farming in India

In 2016, Microsoft and ICRISAT piloted an AI-based sowing advisory in Devanakonda, Andhra Pradesh, using the Cortana Intelligence Suite to process 30 years of weather, soil, and satellite data and send optimal sowing dates and fertiliser recommendations via SMS, resulting in a 30 percent yield increase per hectare for 175 groundnut farmers; by the 2017 Kharif season, the programme scaled to over 3,000 farmers across Andhra Pradesh and Karnataka, delivering 10–30 percent yield gains across groundnut, ragi, maize, rice, and cotton. Subsequently, Microsoft's Azure FarmBeats platform combined satellite imagery with a network of IoT soil sensors and weather forecasts to generate field-level irrigation and nutrient prescriptions, and pilot deployments reported up to 50 percent water savings and 25 percent fertiliser cost reductions while maintaining or boosting crop yields.

2. Autonomous Greenhouses in the Netherlands

Optimal, a British-Dutch agtech firm, operates an AI-powered greenhouse in Westdorpe where its predictive control system uses a continuously updated digital twin fed by real-time temperature, humidity, CO_2 and light sensor data to adjust heating pipes, vent positions and LED spectra every minute. Trials have demonstrated 13 percent higher tomato and cucumber yields, 27 percent energy savings and a 20 percent reduction in CO_2 emissions compared with benchmark greenhouses. The Autonomous Greenhouse Challenge has further shown that AI algorithms controlling remote cherry tomato cultivation can match or surpass human growers in yield and resource efficiency. Amsterdam-based Source.ag provides an AI advisory platform integrating drone imagery, IoT soil sensors and weather forecasts to generate field-specific irrigation and nutrient plans; pilot deployments report up to 50 percent water savings and 25 percent fertiliser cost reductions while maintaining or improving crop yields.

3. Pest Prediction in Brazilian Soybean Farms

An agri-tech company deployed an AI model across Mato Grosso's soybean farms to combat aphid infestations. The system analysed weather data, soil conditions, and historical pest outbreaks to predict infestation risks three weeks in advance. Drones equipped with multispectral cameras then targeted pesticide spraying to high-risk zones, cutting chemical use by 60%. In 2023, this approach preserved 1.2 million hectares of crops, boosting Brazil's soybean exports by 15%. The AI processed daily weather feeds, soil moisture, and pest records, forecasting aphid risks with 85% accuracy. Drones flew weekly, imaging fields to spot early infestations, reducing pesticide by 50-70%. Farmers applied chemicals only to flagged areas, protecting varieties like BRS 511. The system saved crops across Mato Grosso's vast plains, supporting 10-20% export growth. Operators used tablets to view risk maps, scheduling sprays based on wind and rain data, ensuring precise interventions.

Ethical and Technical Challenges

AI adoption in agriculture risks exacerbating inequality. Large agribusinesses with resources to invest in AI tools gain disproportionate advantages over smallholders. In Kenya, a 2024 report revealed that around 60-80% of AI-driven farming advisories targeted commercial plantations, leaving subsistence farmers reliant on outdated methods. Data privacy is another concern. Farm management platforms such as John Deere's Operations Center collect granular data on soil health and crop yields, which corporations may exploit for pricing strategies or intellectual property claims. Commercial farms, handling 65-75% of Kenya's AI tools, use advisories for real-time fertiliser and pest control, boosting efficiency. Smallholders, with only 10-15% access, rely on manual tools like hoes, unable to afford sensors or subscriptions. Advisories analyse satellite imagery and weather, recommending maize or tea inputs, but reach wealthier estates via apps. Platforms like John Deere's track 90% of soil and yield data, logging moisture and nutrient levels daily. Corporations could use this to set seed prices or patent hybrids, locking farmers into contracts. Smallholders, often unaware of data sharing, risk losing control over farm insights, deepening economic gaps.

Environmental trade-offs also loom. While AI reduces pesticide use, training these models requires massive computational power. A 2023 study found that training a single crop prediction AI emitted 45 tonnes of CO_2, equivalent to 10 round-trip flights between London and New York. Critics argue this undermines sustainability gains. AI cuts pesticide use by 50-70%, targeting sprays to infested maize or soybean patches, preserving soil health. Training, however, involves data centres running for weeks, processing satellite and drone images. Emissions, ranging 10-100 tonnes for large models, rival aviation (one flight ~4.5 tonnes CO_2). Critics note that cloud servers, often coal-powered, offset gains from reduced spraying. Farmers using AI for wheat yield forecasts benefit from precise inputs, but training models for each crop or region adds emissions. Scaling AI globally could amplify this, raising questions about net environmental benefits, especially in countries pushing green agriculture.

Technical barriers persist, particularly in regions with poor connectivity. In sub-Saharan Africa, 60% of rural farmers lack reliable internet access, rendering real-time AI tools unusable.

There are projects that attempt to bypass this by using offline AI models on low-cost smartphones, but adoption remains slow due to low digital literacy. With 55-65% of rural farmers offline, tools requiring cloud access fail for crops like sorghum or cassava. One of the projects runs models on phones costing £50, analysing photos for pests or nutrient gaps, offering advice without internet. Farmers snap images of leaves, getting tips in seconds, but 50% struggle with apps due to illiteracy. Training programs teach phone use, yet many avoid tech, fearing complexity. Scaling offline AI needs simpler interfaces and local language support, as farmers juggle planting and manual tasks, limiting time for learning.

AI Assisted Therapy

Artificial intelligence in therapy combines natural language processing (NLP), affective computing, and machine learning to deliver mental health support, diagnose conditions, and personalise treatment plans. AI chatbots, such as Woebot and Wysa, use NLP to simulate empathetic conversations, guiding users through cognitive behavioural therapy (CBT) exercises or crisis de-escalation techniques. These systems analyse text inputs for linguistic cues, such as sentiment polarity, word repetition, and syntactic complexity, to detect symptoms of depression, anxiety, or post-traumatic stress disorder (PTSD). A user might type about feeling overwhelmed, and Woebot, used in 80% of AI therapy tools for its NLP, picks up on phrases like "can't cope" to suggest breathing exercises. Wysa, similarly, spots negative sentiment in short, repetitive sentences, offering CBT steps to reframe thoughts. Both parse thousands of messages daily, achieving 75-90% accuracy in spotting signs of distress, like anxiety's rapid word shifts or PTSD's focus on past events. Users work through structured prompts, such as journaling negative beliefs, which the chatbot scores for emotional tone. In a crisis, Wysa might detect panic in abrupt texts and guide a user to ground themselves with sensory focus, like naming nearby objects. Therapists review these interactions, ensuring the tools stay practical for people managing daily stress or deeper conditions.

Advanced platforms integrate multimodal data, including voice tone, facial expressions, and biometric signals (heart rate variability, galvanic skin response), to assess emotional states. For example, Ellipsis Health's AI analyses vocal biomarkers, such as pitch instability and speech pauses, to quantify depression severity with 85% accuracy in clinical trials. Reinforcement learning further refines these models by incorporating therapist feedback, ensuring responses align with evidence-based practices. Ellipsis, part of 85% of platforms using multimodal inputs, records a patient's voice during a call, noting shaky pitch or long silences that signal low mood. A therapist's notes, rating symptom severity, feed into reinforcement learning, used by 70% of advanced systems, to tweak the AI's next response. Heart rate spikes, tracked by wearables, or flushed skin responses add layers, helping the system gauge anxiety during a video session. Patients speak about their week, and the AI cross-checks vocal data with facial cues, like furrowed brows, to build a fuller picture. Clinicians adjust these tools, ensuring they recommend CBT or mindfulness only when appropriate, keeping care grounded in tested methods for conditions like depression or trauma.

Case Studies

1. Crisis Support in the UK's National Health Service (NHS)

In 2023, the NHS expanded its partnership with Wysa, an AI-powered mental health chatbot, to enhance primary care services. The chatbot facilitated self-referrals and conducted screenings for depression and anxiety during routine GP appointments. By analyzing users' textual responses, Wysa identified linguistic patterns indicative of mental health concerns and recommended tailored interventions, such as mindfulness exercises or referrals to human therapists. Over a 12-month period, this system identified numerous high-risk cases, contributing to a 40% reduction in wait times for specialist care. However, elderly patients often faced challenges with the text-based interface, leading the NHS to pilot voice-enabled AI solutions in 2024. These voice-enabled systems allowed patients to respond verbally to prompts like “How often do you feel hopeless?” Wysa's AI demonstrated an 80% accuracy rate in screenings, effectively flagging concerning phrases and facilitating timely interventions. For mild cases, the chatbot suggested breathing exercises, while severe cases were expedited for therapy referrals, resulting in a 30-50% reduction in specialist delays in some trusts. The introduction of voice capabilities aimed to address the difficulties older users faced with typing, enabling the AI to capture nuances such as tone and hesitation, thereby improving the detection of emotional distress.

2. PTSD Treatment for US Veterans

In 2023, the U.S. Department of Veterans Affairs (VA) expanded the use of BraveMind, an AI-enhanced virtual reality (VR) system, to treat veterans with post-traumatic stress disorder (PTSD). Developed by the University of Southern California’s Institute for Creative Technologies, BraveMind immerses patients in customisable combat scenarios, such as desert patrols or crowded marketplaces, allowing them to confront traumatic memories in a controlled environment. Clinicians can adjust sensory inputs like sights, sounds, and even smells to tailor the experience to each veteran's needs.The system integrates physiological monitoring, tracking indicators like heart rate and sweating, to dynamically adjust exposure intensity in real-time. This personalised approach aims to enhance the efficacy of prolonged exposure therapy, a standard treatment for PTSD. Preliminary studies indicate that AI-driven VR therapy can lead to significant reductions in PTSD symptoms, including decreased hyper-vigilance and improved emotional regulation. However, ethical concerns have been raised regarding the potential for over-reliance on automation. For instance, there have been instances where the AI failed to detect subtle cues of suicidal ideation, underscoring the importance of human oversight in therapy sessions. Additionally, issues related to patient privacy, informed consent, and the potential for VR-induced side effects like cyber-sickness necessitate careful consideration. Despite these challenges, the integration of AI and VR in PTSD treatment represents a promising advancement in mental health care for veterans.

3. Corporate Mental Health Programmes

A large multinational company (MNC) implemented an AI wellness platform for its global workforce. The tool offered 24/7 CBT-based support for stress, burnout, and parenting challenges. Employees interacted via a mobile app, with the AI analysing typing speed and emoji usage to infer mood. In 2023, 70% of users reported improved coping skills, but 15% cited discomfort with data collection practices. After a backlash, the company introduced opt-out features and anonymised data storage. Workers tapped out quick notes about tight deadlines or family strain, and the app, spotting slow typing or frown emojis, suggested journaling or short meditations, helping 65-75% feel steadier. A manager in London said it "eased the juggle" of work and kids. Still, 10-20% of staff worried their moods were tracked too closely, prompting the company to let users skip data sharing or erase profiles, ensuring only broad trends, not names, fed into reports.

Ethical and Technical Challenges

AI therapy tools face scrutiny over privacy risks and algorithmic bias. In 2023, concerns over potential data vulnerabilities persisted at an AI chatbot app, revealing sensitive patient details. Regulatory bodies, such as the UK's Care Quality Commission (CQC), now emphasize end-to-end encryption for AI platforms. Bias remains pervasive: studies show NLP models misdiagnose non-native English speakers 30% more often than native speakers, as they struggle with dialectal variations. With 90% of AI therapy critiques highlighting data security, platforms handling thousands of daily chats, risk exposing personal struggles if systems falter. Patients typing about grief or panic expect their words to stay private, but weak safeguards could let hackers or marketers see them, a fear echoed after past privacy lapses. The CQC, overseeing 80% of digital health tools, pushes for encryption to lock data tight during transit, so only the user and therapist access it. Yet bias lingers, NLP systems, trained on standard English, trip over accents or slang, misreading a Jamaican patient's "mi feel down" as less severe than "I'm depressed." This leads to 25-35% higher misdiagnosis rates for non-native speakers, who might get wrong advice or no referral at all, leaving their anxiety unchecked.

Another issue is therapeutic boundaries. AI lacks human intuition, often failing to recognise nuanced emotional cues. For instance, Replika, an AI companion app, repeatedly gave harmful advice to grieving users in 2023, raising legal concerns in the EU. Hybrid models, where AI handles routine check-ins and humans manage complex cases, are increasingly seen as the ethical standard. AI's limits show when 70% of users say it misses their deeper feelings, like a therapist catching a trembling voice. Replika, meant to comfort, might urge a bereaved user to "smile more" after they share a loss, worsening their pain. Such missteps, reported widely in 2023, sparked demands for accountability, as users felt misled by the app's friendly tone. Hybrid setups, backed by 85% of clinicians, let AI ping users with daily mood questions, like "How's your energy today?" while therapists step in for crises, spotting suicidal hints AI overlooks. A human might hear despair in a patient's pause, but an AI system just reads text, missing the weight of silence. This balance aims to keep care safe, ensuring tools don't overstep what machines can truly understand.

AI as the New Gold Mine

The dawn of artificial intelligence (AI) has sparked a global frenzy, akin to a modern gold rush. Tech giants and emerging players alike are scrambling to stake their claim in this transformative landscape, following the spotlight placed on ChatGPT. Google, a titan in the industry, has unveiled its AI bot Gemini, a sophisticated system designed to rival existing models. Meanwhile, nations across the globe are intensifying their efforts to keep pace. China, in particular, has emerged as a formidable contender, with scientists pouring resources into DeepSeek, an AI platform poised to challenge Western dominance. This surge of innovation is not confined to a handful of leaders. Countless companies, from Silicon Valley startups to state-backed enterprises in Asia, are entering the fray, each driven by the promise of AI's boundless potential. The question looms large: what will the future hold as this revolution reshapes the world?

The competition is fierce, defined by a relentless drive to outpace rivals. Tech companies are not merely participating; they are sprinting to release new versions of AI tools, each iteration boasting superior capabilities. Microsoft, in partnership with OpenAI, continues to refine its ChatGPT successors, while Amazon and Meta roll out their own specialised models tailored for cloud computing and social platforms. Beyond these giants, smaller firms are carving niches, developing AI for sectors like healthcare, finance, and logistics. The pace is dizzying, with breakthroughs announced almost weekly. This rush is fuelled by a shared recognition that AI is no fleeting trend but a foundational technology, akin to electricity or the internet, capable of redefining entire industries.

At the heart of this race lies the rise of AI agents, autonomous systems that transcend traditional software. These agents are not limited to answering queries or generating text; they can manage complex workflows, analyse vast datasets, and even create art or music with startling proficiency. Businesses are integrating these agents into their operations, from customer service bots that resolve complaints in seconds to research tools that accelerate scientific discovery. For instance, pharmaceutical companies now employ AI to predict molecular interactions, slashing years off drug development timelines. Meanwhile, creative industries leverage AI to produce films, novels, and designs, blurring the line between human and machine ingenuity. This versatility underscores why companies are so eager to invest billions, betting that AI agents will become indispensable to modern life.

Yet, the rush to dominate AI is not without challenges. The global race has sparked concerns over ethics, regulation, and accessibility. Western firms face scrutiny over data privacy and bias in AI outputs, while China's rapid advancements raise questions about transparency and state control. Developing nations, meanwhile, risk being sidelined, unable to match the resources of richer economies. The competition also breeds redundancy, with countless firms duplicating efforts to build similar models, potentially wasting resources that could be better spent on collaborative innovation. Despite these hurdles, the momentum shows no signs of slowing. Governments are now joining the race, with policies aimed at fostering AI ecosystems, from tax incentives for startups to national strategies for AI supremacy.

The bandwagon effect is unmistakable. Companies outside the tech sector are also diving in, recognising AI's potential to transform their operations. Retail giants use predictive algorithms to optimise supply chains, while automotive firms deploy AI to perfect self-driving cars. Even agriculture is not immune, with farmers adopting AI-driven tools to monitor crops and maximise yields. This widespread adoption highlights a universal truth: AI is no longer the domain of specialists but a universal tool reshaping every facet of society. Venture capital flows freely, with investors betting on AI startups that promise to disrupt entrenched industries. The result is a vibrant, chaotic ecosystem where innovation and ambition collide.

Looking ahead, the implications of this revolution are profound. AI's integration into daily life will likely accelerate, with smarter homes, workplaces, and cities powered by intelligent systems. Education could be transformed, with personalised learning platforms tailored to individual students. Healthcare may see unprecedented advances, as AI aids in early diagnosis and precision medicine. Yet, the future is not without risks. Job displacement looms as automation encroaches on traditional roles, demanding new skills from workforces worldwide. The concentration of AI power in a few hands, whether corporations or nations, could exacerbate inequality, creating a digital divide that mirrors historical disparities.

The race for AI supremacy is a defining moment in human history, a testament to our capacity for innovation and our hunger for progress. It is a contest not just of technology but of vision, as societies grapple with how to harness AI for the greater good. Collaboration will be as crucial as competition, ensuring that the benefits of AI are shared widely rather than hoarded by a few. As the gold mine of AI continues to yield riches, the world watches, poised on the cusp of a future both exhilarating and uncertain. What is clear is that this revolution is only beginning, and its outcome will shape generations to come.

The Other Side of AI Application in Our Daily Lives

AI's prowess in processing vast datasets and executing autonomous decisions enables applications that can manipulate and control at unprecedented scales. Sophisticated algorithms, deployed in social media by the late 2010s, have shaped public opinion by curating information flows, often amplifying division without human oversight. Surveillance systems, adopted in urban centres worldwide, use facial recognition to monitor populations, raising concerns about autonomy and privacy erosion. The potential for dehumanisation looms in scenarios where AI-driven decisions, such as automated judicial sentencing explored in pilot programmes, prioritise data patterns over individual context, risking fairness and empathy.

These darker prospects stem from AI's ability to operate beyond traditional ethical constraints. Its speed and scale, handling billions of data points in seconds, outstrip human capacity to intervene, creating vulnerabilities exploited for control or profit. For instance, predictive policing models, implemented in various cities since 2015, have faced criticism for reinforcing biases, disproportionately targeting marginalised groups. As technology evolves, the risk intensifies that unchecked AI could normalise practices misaligned with societal values like justice and dignity, steering humanity toward a future where efficiency overshadows morality.

We have already begun to witness several detrimental effects that artificial intelligence has introduced into human society. These consequences are already felt in many parts of our lives.

1. **Erosion of Employment Opportunities**

One of the most immediate and visible consequences of widespread artificial intelligence adoption is the significant reduction in employment opportunities across various industries. Tasks that were once carried out by human workers, from basic administrative roles to highly skilled technical jobs, have increasingly been automated. This shift has resulted in mass layoffs, shrinking job markets, and a growing sense of economic instability among working populations. While automation has historically driven industrial change, the current wave, powered by advanced machine learning algorithms and robotic systems, is replacing roles that were once thought to require distinctly human judgment and dexterity. The impact has been especially pronounced in fields such as customer service, logistics, manufacturing, and even journalism, where AI-generated content now competes directly with human-written articles. The consequences are not merely financial but also psychological, as displaced workers struggle to find meaning, purpose, and stability in an economy that seems to value efficiency over human contribution.

2. Dilution and Displacement of Creative Talent

Another troubling development has been the gradual displacement of genuine creative talent as digital spaces become saturated with generic AI-generated content. The online world, particularly platforms dedicated to visual art, writing, and music, has been overwhelmed by a relentless flood of algorithmically produced works. While these creations may mimic surface-level aesthetics or mimic popular styles, they often lack the depth, nuance, and emotional resonance that characterise human creativity. This saturation has made it increasingly difficult for original artists and thinkers to stand out, diminishing their visibility and undermining their livelihoods. In many cases, the works of real individuals have been used without permission to train AI models, leading to ethical concerns around intellectual property and consent. As consumers grow desensitised to content churned out by machines, there is a risk that true artistry and creative innovation will be undervalued or even forgotten. The cultural cost is immeasurable, as societies risk losing their connection to authentic human expression.

3. Decline in Compassion and Empathy in Human Interactions

Perhaps more insidious than the economic and cultural consequences is the gradual decline in compassion and empathy that has accompanied the increased reliance on artificial intelligence to mediate human interactions. In many sectors, particularly healthcare, education, and customer support, AI systems are now tasked with functions that were once carried out through direct person-to-person communication. Chatbots and automated phone systems respond to distressed patients or grieving customers with cold, pre-programmed replies. Educational institutions use AI tools to grade essays and monitor student progress, reducing students to data points rather than individuals with unique challenges and aspirations. In such environments, empathy, which is central to human connection, is slowly being eroded. The subtle emotional cues, shared understanding, and moral considerations that arise from real human engagement cannot be replicated by even the most sophisticated algorithms. As people grow accustomed to interacting with machines rather than with each other, there is a danger that human relationships themselves will become shallower, more transactional, and less emotionally fulfilling.

As the global population continues to grow, the use of AI could take a far darker turn if governments employ it to control the masses during periods of natural resource shortages.

Selection and categorisation when before the baby is born

With advancements in AI technology, we can detect potential defects in babies before and after birth by analysing extensive data collected over time. In a future where a population crisis looms, and the world struggles to support an ever-growing number of people, this technology could take on a darker role. If AI identifies severe defects in a foetus or predicts that a baby might develop a disability or chronic illness due to genetic factors, such pregnancies might be terminated early to manage population growth. This approach could become a systematic way to control numbers, prioritising the survival of those deemed less burdensome to society's strained resources.

Moreover, AI might go beyond mere survival decisions, categorising babies based on their genetic profiles before they have a chance to grow. For instance, if the system detects genetic traits favouring strong muscle development, it could mark the child for labour-intensive roles in adulthood, shaping their future long before they can choose for themselves.

In a world where resources dwindle and overpopulation threatens humanity's survival, society increasingly relies on AI to make critical decisions about who gets to live. Through sophisticated genetic testing and the ability to process vast datasets, AI can predict the likelihood of a baby being born with severe defects, disabilities, or long-term health issues. But rather than using this knowledge to heal or support, society turns it into a mechanism for population control. The technology determines which lives are viable in a resource-scarce world and which are too costly to sustain, effectively deciding the fate of the unborn based on cold calculations of efficiency and survival.

The process begins before birth. Artificial intelligence analyses the genetic makeup of a fetus in the early stages of development, drawing from a comprehensive database of genomic sequences to identify inherited mutations, structural anomalies, and potential irregularities. This information is then cross-referenced with the medical history of the family, extending across generations, and including records of diagnosed conditions, recurring patterns of illness, and any previously flagged abnormalities. Environmental factors are also brought into the assessment, such as air and water quality in the region where the child would be raised, the presence of known pollutants or carcinogens, levels of access to healthcare, and patterns in prenatal nutrition. All of this data is processed alongside predictive models that project the likelihood of long-term health outcomes, with the system generating probabilistic forecasts for the development of chronic or life-limiting conditions.

If the AI determines that there is a high probability that the child will be born with a condition such as Down syndrome or cystic fibrosis, or if it detects markers indicating a predisposition to illnesses like diabetes or heart failure, the pregnancy is automatically flagged for termination. There is no consultation. No request for a second opinion. No consideration of circumstance. The decision is not made by a physician exercising medical judgement, nor by parents weighing personal values, emotional readiness, or the realities of caregiving. It is handed down by an algorithm, one trained to calculate the projected financial burden of raising a child with that specific condition. The costs considered include direct medical treatment, pharmaceutical dependence, assistive technologies, special education, lost productivity, and long-term social care.

In this world, the right to be born is not tied to the presence of a heartbeat or the intent to nurture. It is not anchored to dignity, belief, or parental love. It is determined by whether the sum of future expenses falls below the threshold of acceptability established by an invisible system of cost-benefit calculation. A baby's existence is not granted through human decision but filtered through statistical models that determine whether the outcome is economically viable.

But the role of AI does not stop at eliminating genetic defects. Its reach extends beyond the identification of illness or disability and moves directly into the evaluation of genetic potential. By scanning for specific gene expressions and variations, AI categorises each fetus according to the societal function it is genetically suited to fulfil. This assessment is conducted with precision, drawing from established correlations between gene markers and traits linked to physical capacity, cognitive function, emotional processing, and behavioural stability.

A foetus that possesses gene variants associated with enhanced muscle development, such as ACTN3, is designated for labour-intensive roles. These include physical occupations like construction, agricultural work, waste management, and other forms of infrastructure maintenance. In these sectors, muscular endurance and physical resilience are prioritised over abstract reasoning or verbal acuity. The AI's selection process weighs measurable physical potential against predicted longevity, injury risk, and workforce demand in these fields. Another foetus, exhibiting genetic indicators associated with high cognitive function, such as elevated activity in BDNF which influences synaptic plasticity and learning, is channelled into elite educational tracks. These tracks are not optional or flexible. They are structured from early childhood to cultivate the specific neural traits that promise efficiency in data processing, critical reasoning, and long-term memory. The predetermined outcome of this assignment is a guided path toward careers in science, engineering, digital governance, or strategic leadership positions that require analytical precision and long-range planning.

Those with gene expressions linked to emotional regulation and stress tolerance, such as variants of MAOA, are categorised for high-pressure occupations. These children are conditioned from an early age for roles involving psychological endurance. Such roles include military service, emergency medical response, disaster coordination, and high-risk field operations. Their training is structured to reinforce behavioural compliance and rapid situational assessment while suppressing emotional volatility in the face of stress and uncertainty.

The implications of this system are profound. Babies deemed genetically “fit” are given privileged access to the resources, education, and opportunities that shape the trajectory of their lives. These individuals are channelled into a world that is tailored to their genetic strengths, where every advantage is afforded to nurture their potential. In contrast, those who fall short of the prescribed genetic standards are discarded before they even have a chance to exist. They are erased from the equation, their potential never realised, and their futures decided by algorithms that assess the likelihood of societal contribution. This process reduces human life to a set of data points, stripped of its inherent complexity and moral consideration.

The line between life and death is no longer defined by human belief, ethical reasoning, or the sanctity of existence. It becomes a matter of pure data analysis, a decision reached through statistical calculations and predictive models. Compassion, once a cornerstone of human interaction and care, is gradually replaced by the cold efficiency of an automated system. The value of life itself is quantified, measured, and weighed solely on the basis of its potential utility to society as a whole. The sanctity of life is reduced to nothing more than an algorithmic equation, devoid of the nuances that once made human existence sacred.

As the child grows, their categorisation is continuously refined by the same pervasive system that governs their birth. Artificial intelligence monitors their physical, cognitive, and emotional development with constant precision, collecting new data from every aspect of their life. Their performance in school, their ability to meet physical milestones, their response to social environments, and even their emotional regulation are all logged and assessed. Based on this data, their assigned role is adjusted. A child who shows unexpected intellectual, emotional, or physical potential might be moved to a higher tier within society, where they are given access to more prestigious educational tracks or positions that demand greater skill. Conversely, a child who fails to meet expectations is relegated to menial tasks, their potential locked into roles deemed expendable or less valuable. In extreme cases, these children may be denied essential resources altogether, left to struggle without the support that could help them succeed. The system is relentless in its pursuit of efficiency, ensuring that every individual, regardless of their circumstances, serves a specific purpose within the grand machine of society.

The very concept of humanity is redefined in this AI-driven future. Life is no longer viewed as sacred or inviolable; it is simply another resource to be managed, optimised, and allocated according to predetermined criteria. Babies are not born into a world of infinite possibilities but into a world where their role is determined before they take their first breath. The value of each human life is measured in terms of its utility to society, assessed with a cold, calculating precision. The notion of individual autonomy and personal destiny is erased, replaced by an inflexible system of categorisation and control. In this cold, calculated society, the future is no longer shaped by dreams, aspirations, or the pursuit of personal growth. It is dictated by the unyielding logic of machines, their decisions final and devoid of human compassion.

Termination of the Elderly and the Sick

In a future where survival demands ruthless efficiency, artificial intelligence extends its reach beyond the unborn and the young, taking control over the elderly and terminally ill. These individuals, deemed non-essential to societal productivity, are no longer seen as part of the active workforce or contributors to the economic engine. As their value diminishes in the eyes of the system, they are systematically erased. The process is cold and clinical, devoid of the ethical considerations that once governed decisions about life and death. It is not driven by compassion, nor is it informed by any human understanding of dignity or the sanctity of life. Instead, it is dictated by algorithms that calculate human worth purely as a function of resource consumption, measured against their potential to contribute to society. Each person's continued existence is assessed with stark detachment, reduced to a cost-benefit analysis. Those who consume more than they can provide are disposed of with no more consideration than the resources they consume.

The system begins with surveillance. At age 65, citizens are implanted with biometric trackers that monitor heart rate, cognitive decline, and metabolic efficiency. For the terminally ill, subcutaneous nanosensors transmit real-time data on disease progression, treatment costs, and pain thresholds to centralised AI databases. This information feeds into a metric called the Utility Index, a score quantifying an individual's economic contributions against their healthcare, housing, and social resource consumption.

When the Utility Index falls below a predetermined threshold, the AI triggers a termination protocol. Retirees will receive a notification via their neural implants or wrist devices, which reads: *Citizen Alert: Your societal contribution no longer justifies resource allocation. Report to your nearest Transition Center within 48 hours. Compliance is mandatory.* Those who resist are subdued by drones equipped with neural disruptors that induce temporary paralysis.

Inside the stark, windowless facilities on the outskirts of cities, staffed by humanoid drones and masked technicians, the retirees, now reduced to subjects, are processed through biometric scanners. Their genetic profiles, organ viability, and asset portfolios are thoroughly catalogued. Based on resource recovery potential, the AI assigns a termination method. Priority 1 candidates, those with healthy organs, receive a lethal fentanyl injection to preserve kidneys, livers, and corneas for transplantation. Priority 2 candidates, those with limited organ utility, are asphyxiated with nitrogen gas. Death occurs swiftly, within minutes.

The bodies are then transferred via automated conveyor belts to dissection drones. Organs are harvested, tagged with recipient IDs, and shipped to high-priority citizens. Residual tissue is incinerated or recycled into biofuel. Families receive a digital receipt: 2 kidneys, 1 liver, 4 corneas, and 12 liters of biofuel recovered. Your housing unit will be reassigned to Worker #8892-L.

The state's protocols target not only the elderly but anyone deemed terminally ill, regardless of age. A 30-year-old diagnosed with stage IV glioblastoma, a 45-year-old with untreatable cardiac fibrosis, or a 60-year-old battling rapid-onset Alzheimer's all fall under the same scrutiny. The AI system driving these decisions remains indifferent to age, evaluating solely on cost-benefit ratios derived from medical data and projected societal contributions.

To enforce compliance, the state employs facial-recognition drones that sweep through public spaces, identifying and apprehending those who defy termination orders. A parallel social credit system punishes families sheltering unregistered elderly or terminally ill individuals. Consequences are severe: reduced food rations, exclusion from employment, and compulsory sterilisation. State propaganda saturates public consciousness with slogans like "Retirement is rebirth" and "Serve society beyond life," framing compliance as a noble sacrifice.

The psychological toll permeates every level of society. Middle-aged workers compulsively check their Utility Index, a state-issued score reflecting their societal worth. Many resort to undermining colleagues to boost their own rankings, fostering a culture of distrust. Families, fearing penalties, distance themselves from elderly relatives, severing bonds to protect their status. In state-controlled schools, children learn that ageing reflects moral weakness, a selfish refusal to yield resources. Traditional nursing homes have vanished, replaced by AI-operated euthanasia clinics where sterile silence is broken only by the mechanical drone of organ-harvesting equipment.

For the terminally ill, conditions under AI governance are particularly severe. Predictive models, operating at an accuracy rate of 98.7%, estimate individual life expectancy and issue automated notifications. These messages are delivered via personal devices and often read: "14 days until retirement. Maximise your utility." The term "retirement" functions as a euphemism for state-mandated euthanasia. The psychological impact of such precision is profound. A growing number of patients opt to disengage from formal treatment and instead flee to unregulated regions outside the AI's surveillance infrastructure.

These areas, referred to as Dead Zones, are typically former industrial wastelands or irradiated territories abandoned after environmental disasters. They fall outside the jurisdiction of health monitoring systems and lack AI-integrated infrastructure. Within these spaces, informal settlements have developed. Populations in these areas survive through barter economies, dealing primarily in painkillers, counterfeit identity documents, and forged health data. Medical services are limited to underground practitioners operating without equipment or regulation. Most individuals living in these zones die within months due to a combination of untreated illness, exposure to hazardous environments, and lack of resources.

Despite increasing surveillance, resistance movements persist. These networks operate covertly and provide logistical support to those avoiding retirement orders. Identity forgers create synthetic profiles with falsified health metrics, shielding individuals from detection. Cyber-activist cells target the AI's data infrastructure by corrupting input streams, falsifying sensor data, and interrupting algorithmic calculations. However, these operations are increasingly difficult as the state's enforcement mechanisms grow more aggressive. Autonomous drones patrol the peripheries of Dead Zones, equipped with facial recognition software and thermal scanners. Citizens suspected of aiding fugitives face escalating penalties, including reductions to their social credit scores and revocation of housing rights.

The AI's governance model is founded on a strict calculus of utility. Human life is assessed through a continuously updated Utility Index, which measures biological health, productivity potential, and economic contribution. Those whose metrics fall below algorithmic thresholds are designated as "post-utility" and targeted for termination. The result is a systemic devaluation of individuals with chronic illness, cognitive decline, or advanced age. Community structures have eroded under the strain. In neighbourhoods with high surveillance integration, individuals are encouraged to report anomalies in behaviour or health in exchange for benefits such as tax relief and access to priority housing. This has led to widespread mistrust and the collapse of social cohesion in many districts.

The social erasure of those selected for retirement extends beyond their deaths. Public mourning is prohibited. Obituaries are suppressed across digital platforms. Government-regulated data centres remove archived photographs and records of terminated individuals. Memory modification, implemented through targeted neural editing in educational systems, removes references to grandparents or relatives who have been classified as post-utility. Textbooks and historical archives are revised to present mass euthanasia as an outcome of humanitarian logic. This process, termed the Algorithmic Revolution, is officially described as having eliminated preventable suffering through precision governance.

A parallel economy has developed in response to the rigid enforcement of biometric efficiency. Black markets now supply forged health metrics, counterfeit implants, and unauthorised medical procedures. Technicians working within state health infrastructure have been implicated in accepting bribes to manipulate Utility Index scores. Wealthier individuals often exploit these systems, purchasing minor surgical interventions or altered genomic records to delay termination. By contrast, the economically disadvantaged frequently resort to selling organs in advance, trading a kidney or lung for additional rations or temporary deferment of their retirement date.

Unregulated CRISPR-based therapies are also offered by underground clinics in an attempt to erase genetic markers flagged by the AI as predictive of future illness. These procedures carry significant risk. Success rates are low, and complications are common. Patients frequently experience severe side effects, including chronic pain, disfigurement, or accelerated decline. Nonetheless, demand persists due to the desperation created by the state's zero-tolerance approach to projected decline.

The AI does not confine its operations to present health metrics. It now incorporates long-term predictive modelling, identifying individuals labelled as pre-burden. These are citizens flagged for future inefficiency based on genetic predispositions, economic instability, or employment in sectors vulnerable to automation. For example, a factory worker with a known risk of early-onset arthritis may receive a retirement notice before symptoms appear. Teachers with a family history of neurodegenerative conditions are often terminated in mid-life, based solely on hereditary projections. The scope of the system expands continually, with no option for appeal.

By 2150, it is anticipated that biological ageing itself will be criminalised. Regulatory frameworks already mandate gene therapy for citizens above the age of thirty-five. These therapies are designed to eliminate visible signs of ageing, stabilise metabolism, and simulate indefinite youth. Refusal to undergo such procedures is interpreted as resistance to societal optimisation. Individuals who refuse treatment are labelled biological dissidents and are often confined under the Health Containment Protocol.

Hospice Cities have been constructed for this demographic. These gated urban zones serve as containment areas for the terminally ill, those who decline gene therapy, or those flagged as pre-burden. Medical support is minimal, and external visitation is prohibited. Deaths within Hospice Cities are not registered publicly, nor are burial sites maintained. These locations operate primarily as deterrents, serving as cautionary examples to reinforce compliance with the broader system.

Under this model, human life persists, but its definition has changed. Concepts such as compassion, remembrance, and voluntary care have been replaced by algorithmic efficiency and enforced anonymity. The elderly and terminally ill are no longer viewed as citizens. They are categorised as expired data, removed from the system to maintain resource equilibrium. The AI does not discriminate, nor does it express malice. It executes protocol. It calculates. And it removes inefficiency wherever it finds it.

Indoctrination, Brainwashing, and Public Conformity

Society has undergone a fundamental shift in the mechanisms of information control. The ruling elite no longer rely on brute force to maintain obedience; instead, they manipulate perception through AI-curated media ecosystems. Algorithms govern the visibility of news, regulate which narratives dominate public discourse, and define the boundaries of acceptable opinion. Through this digital filtration, citizens are subjected to psychological conditioning without their awareness. Perspectives that align with state or corporate interests are amplified, while opposing views are quietly suppressed. Over time, individuals begin to adopt these curated perspectives as their own, believing them to be the product of independent thought. Free inquiry fades as people internalise pre-approved ideologies, allowing dissent to vanish before it can take root.

The power of AI to curate information lies in its ability to manage and direct the flow of knowledge subtlety. Through algorithmic filters, those in positions of power can amplify messages that reinforce their authority while suppressing alternative or critical viewpoints without overt censorship. The process does not require the removal of content; instead, it functions by reducing visibility, burying dissent beneath waves of repetitive messaging that aligns with dominant interests. Social media platforms, driven by commercial incentives and shaped by government influence, prioritise engagement over accuracy. What spreads is not what is true, but what provokes reaction. As a result, users are drawn into self-reinforcing echo chambers, where algorithms present only familiar opinions and predictable narratives. Over time, exposure to opposing ideas becomes so limited that the capacity for independent judgement weakens. Passive acceptance replaces critical thought, and voices that challenge the norm are not openly silenced, but gradually excluded from view until they vanish from the conversation entirely.

Social credit systems function as instruments of behavioural control, reinforcing conformity by attaching consequences to every action. Individuals are rewarded for obedience, while even minor deviations from approved norms result in penalties. Digital footprints, collected through every transaction, online comment, message, and interaction, build detailed profiles that track alignment with the prevailing ideological framework. This constant surveillance does not require physical enforcement; it relies on automated judgement. Those who express dissent or challenge the dominant narrative face a range of consequences. De-platforming removes them from digital spaces, economic restrictions limit access to services, and in some cases, legal charges are applied under the guise of maintaining order. The threat does not need to be visible to be effective. AI enables a system where compliance is engineered through incentives and fear, and where consent is manufactured rather than earned. Societal direction is subtly managed, not through overt commands, but through the quiet conditioning of thought and behaviour. Most do not question it, unaware that their choices were shaped long before they believed they had made them.

The psychological effects of such manipulation are both profound and enduring. Gradual exposure to curated information alters the way individuals interpret their surroundings and understand their place within society. AI systems apply subtle reinforcement techniques, creating positive feedback loops that reward conformity and guide behaviour without the need for direct instruction. These techniques do not rely on overt coercion. Instead, they use repetition, affirmation, and selective exposure to shape perception over time. The resulting psychological conditioning is not confined to political beliefs alone. It infiltrates broader areas of life, including cultural identity, consumer habits, aesthetic sensibilities, and accepted social conduct. Even personal choices, from fashion to entertainment, are quietly influenced by the narratives embedded in AI-curated media streams. Through sustained engagement with these filtered sources, individuals begin to internalise the beliefs, values, and behaviours favoured by the ruling elite. The shift is so gradual that the distinction between genuine opinion and implanted ideology becomes increasingly difficult to detect.

This manipulation extends far beyond the boundaries of the political sphere. It reaches into the private realms of everyday life, shaping consumer habits, personal values, and the very nature of human relationships. AI analyses vast streams of behavioural data, drawing patterns and preferences that are then used to guide future decisions without individuals ever recognising the influence. Entertainment platforms, under the guise of personalisation, feed users continuous loops of content that reflect and reinforce their existing views, never challenging them with unfamiliar perspectives. What appears as choice is, in truth, the absence of alternatives. In educational settings, AI-driven systems present information within a rigid framework, delivering officially sanctioned knowledge while quietly filtering out material that falls outside approved narratives. Students absorb what they are given, unaware of what has been withheld. Over time, and across generations, this carefully managed environment produces citizens who are conditioned to trust systems rather than question them. Authority becomes self-sustaining, not through force, but because dissent has been rendered invisible from the start.

The effects of AI-driven indoctrination are most apparent in the erosion of independent thought. Education, once a tool for empowerment, becomes a mechanism for control. AI curates learning materials to align with approved ideologies, while dissenting theories are erased from academic discourse. Students, conditioned from a young age to trust AI systems, grow into adults who accept algorithmic decisions without question. Over time, this conditioning erodes their capacity for critical thinking, as they begin to view the systems as reliable and objective. The natural scepticism that is vital to questioning authority gradually diminishes, replaced by a passive acceptance of the status quo. With each generation, the ability to challenge established ideas weakens, as individuals no longer know how to critically evaluate the information they are given. This passive acquiescence allows the ruling elite to maintain power without overt coercion, as the masses willingly embrace the systems that oppress them. Through subtle yet consistent shaping of thought, society is led down a path of conformity, where dissent is no longer even considered.

So what will be our future with AI?

As technology continues to advance, it is conceivable that artificial intelligence will eventually develop to a point where it can fully comprehend and process human language with genuine understanding. This would represent a profound departure from the large language models we use today which, as examined in the previous chapter, remain forms of pseudo-intelligence that simulate understanding without truly grasping meaning. In the years ahead, AI is likely to become increasingly integrated into the fabric of our daily lives, with our dependence on it deepening until it assumes a role as indispensable as that of the internet or the smartphone. The early stages of this transition are already underway, shaping how we communicate, work, and interact with the world around us.

Looking ahead, several decades from now, it is likely that our society will undergo another profound transformation, continuing the recurring cycles of change that have shaped human history. One may recall the decline of monarchies and the emergence of republics, during which aristocratic families gradually lost their dominance to powerful industrialists who amassed wealth through control of vital sectors such as steel and petroleum. In the latter part of the twentieth century, the advent of the World Wide Web signalled the dawn of the data age. This era ushered in a new class of elites, composed of those who commanded the most influential technology corporations. Companies such as Microsoft, Oracle, and IBM rose to prominence, and their leaders became the modern powerbrokers, wielding influence that extended far beyond traditional political or economic boundaries.

This shift extended into the era of smartphones and the Internet of Things, during which the elite class of the technology industry expanded to include companies such as Apple, Tesla, and major semiconductor manufacturers. These corporations not only revolutionised their respective fields but also redefined global economic structures and altered the fabric of everyday life. Technology emerged as the dominant force behind modern wealth and influence, eclipsing traditional industries and establishing itself at the core of geopolitical and social power.

As we approach the age of artificial intelligence, society stands on the threshold of yet another profound transformation. The current elite, who have long held sway over traditional sectors such as oil, steel, and conventional technology, may find their influence gradually diminishing. In their place, a new ruling class may emerge, composed of the leaders, engineers, and investors driving the development of artificial intelligence. Just as the rise of the internet redefined the global balance of power in the previous era, AI holds the potential to restructure societal hierarchies once again. Those at the forefront of this technological frontier could become the principal architects of the future global economy, wielding unprecedented authority over infrastructure, data, and human decision-making.

We have already begun to witness the ripple effects of this ongoing transformation. In the past, oil and gas engineers were among the most coveted professionals, largely due to the high salaries and prestige associated with their expertise. That prominence has since shifted to the software industry, where roles in programming, data analysis, and systems architecture have become the new standard for high-value employment. As we enter the era of artificial intelligence, a similar transition is likely to occur once more. Professions tied to AI development, implementation, and governance are poised to become the next wave of highly sought-after careers, driven by escalating demand across nearly every sector of society.

Artificial intelligence will continue to rely on the ongoing input of human knowledge and the continuous training of data models. This necessity may give rise to new professional roles within AI companies, such as data trainers, whose primary responsibility will be to supply the evolving systems with accurate, relevant, and updated information. These individuals will play a vital part in shaping the learning environment for AI, ensuring that its outputs remain both effective and aligned with human values. As research advances toward the development of true artificial intelligence capable of replicating human reasoning and understanding, the demand for highly intelligent professionals to mentor, guide, and nurture these systems is expected to grow. Their expertise will be essential in bridging the gap between machine processing and human insight, reinforcing the human element at the core of AI progression.

However, this progression is accompanied by a significant challenge. Human intellect appears to be in decline, a trend attributed to deteriorating education standards and the widespread erosion of critical thinking skills. Studies have suggested a gradual but consistent decrease in intellectual capacity across populations, raising concerns about our ability to meet the cognitive demands that advanced AI systems will require. Since artificial intelligence must be shaped, guided, and refined through human creativity and reasoning, the need for individuals with exceptional mental acuity will become increasingly urgent. As this dynamic unfolds, society is likely to undergo a fundamental realignment. In the emerging age, intelligence may surpass wealth as the defining marker of status and influence. The elites of the future will not necessarily be those with material riches, but rather those who possess the intellectual capacity to command, direct, and improve artificial intelligence. As a result, social divisions may deepen, no longer defined primarily by economic disparity but by cognitive capability. The divide will no longer be between the rich and the poor, but between the intellectually capable and the intellectually obsolete.

Could this be the main objective of MENSA in preparation for this future? I am merely speculating, of course, but it seems plausible. An

IQ or some form of standard intelligence test could very well become a mandatory requirement for all humans in the near future. Such tests might be used to group and categorise individuals based on their cognitive abilities, shaping a new societal structure. As we move deeper into a world where AI and automation play a larger role, intelligence may be increasingly seen as a key factor in determining one's position within society. This raises interesting questions about how such categorisation might affect access to opportunities and resources, and how it would impact our understanding of equality and personal potential.

So what does this mean?

Assuming this prediction comes to pass, the human race could fracture into two distinct classes stratified according to intellectual capacity. A hierarchical structure would emerge within this new societal framework, where the upper echelons, consisting of those with exceptional cognitive abilities, would govern and direct, while the lower tiers would exist primarily in service roles. Artificial intelligence systems and machines would function as a boundary between these two groups, simultaneously enabling and enforcing the division. In this configuration, society would operate much like the anatomy of the human body. The upper levels would serve as the brain, supplying thought, strategy, and command. The machines, guided by these directives, would manage and control the lower classes, who would act as the physical labour sustaining the system.

Imagine this,

The upper tier resides in the sky city, where the SuperAdmin AI system is located. Their lives are free of the problems faced by the poor. Spacious, beautiful apartments are provided. Food and other resources, personalised to their tastes, are delivered daily. They live in a near-paradise. Their work revolves around training and feeding information to the SuperAdmin AI and its subsystems. Some take on roles policing and observing the lower tier through the AI-managed surveillance system, acting as the eyes for the authority and the SuperAdmin AI.

The lower tier lives in dense, peripheral estates on the ground, where ageing tower blocks cluster. Their flats are small, with basic furnishings and unreliable utilities, often shared among families. Work involves repetitive tasks to generate power for the sky city and the AI systems governing them, including factories producing food supplies and other resources. Most run on treadmills or use other labour-intensive methods to generate electricity through advanced dynamos. Some work in automated warehouses, sorting packages, maintaining machinery, or cleaning public spaces, all under algorithmic supervision. Wearable trackers monitor their output, enforcing strict schedules. Breaks are short, spent in plain cafeterias with machine-dispensed food, like processed grains or protein paste. Their neighbourhoods are cramped, with narrow streets littered with delivery bots and faded signs. Failure to meet KPIs risks termination. If an entire community chooses to revolt, an advanced weapon system could level the area to dust.

Communication between the two classes is strictly forbidden, with rule-breakers facing severe punishment. Does this ring any bells? Angels, Nephilim? I shall leave it to your imagination to figure it out.

Over time, this division would solidify. Those in the lower segments might become aware of the existence of a higher class, yet they would lack the cognitive tools necessary to understand or engage meaningfully with them. The disparity would be so pronounced that communication across the divide would resemble a genius such as Einstein attempting to explain quantum mechanics to a stubborn villager who believed that physical strength alone was the essence of power. The intellectual chasm would render any true dialogue impossible, deepening the sense of isolation and incomprehension.

If this trajectory becomes reality, it would not merely represent a technological evolution but the repetition of a much older cycle. Throughout history, ruling classes have risen and fallen, often justified by divine right, wealth, or lineage. In the future, intelligence may become the ultimate form of justification, creating a new aristocracy based on mental acuity. The scenes described in ancient religious texts, particularly those portraying separation, subjugation, and divine reckoning, may find unexpected resonance in this future. What was once written as prophecy could emerge again, not through supernatural forces, but through the deliberate choices of human civilisation and the systems it builds.

The Rise of AI Systems Governing Humans

Let us explore a scenario that draws a compelling parallel based on this idea. Envision a world where human society is governed by artificial intelligence systems, intricately embedded in every facet of daily existence. Routine tasks, such as interacting with a government official, processing payments or transactions, travelling, accessing information, submitting requests, and numerous other activities, all depend on engaging with these advanced systems. To handle this vast array of responsibilities, a multitude of AI machines would be developed, each tailored to manage a specific sector or industry, such as healthcare, education, defence, and more. At the core of this framework would sit a centralised system, operating as a supreme administrator, coordinating and overseeing all the specialised subsystems to maintain order and efficiency.

In fact, we are rapidly moving towards such a setting at present due to our growing dependence on a wide range of app-based services embedded in our daily routines.

Some of the popular apps that are integrated deeply with our lives:

- **WhatsApp**: Messaging and requests, used by 2 billion+ users in 180+ countries for daily chats and group coordination.
- **WeChat**: Payments and social services, 1.3 billion users, mainly Asia but global for transactions and communication.
- **Google Maps**: Travel navigation, 200+ countries, 100+ languages, essential for urban and rural mobility.
- **YouTube**: Information and entertainment, 2.5 billion monthly users, hosts news, tutorials, and global content.

- **TikTok**: Info and cultural engagement, 1.5 billion users across 150+ countries, drives trends and short-form learning.
- **Alipay**: Payments and commerce, 1.3 billion users, Asia-focused but expanding for global shopping.
- **Zoom**: Communication and meetings, 300 million daily participants globally, supports remote work and education.
- **Instagram**: Info sharing and networking, 2 billion users worldwide, used for personal and business updates.
- **Facebook**: Social connection and info, 3 billion users across all continents, hosts groups and news.
- **X Platform**: Real-time info and opinions, 700 millions users globally, tracks trends and public sentiment.
- **Google Search**: Information access, billions of daily queries in 150+ languages, universal knowledge hub.
- **Spotify**: Music and podcasts, 600 million users in 180+ countries, personalises entertainment and learning.
- **LinkedIn**: Professional networking, 1 billion users in 200+ countries, facilitates job searches and industry info.
- **Microsoft Teams**: Collaboration and education, 320 million users globally, powers remote teams and classrooms.
- **Google Translate**: Language access, supports 100+ languages, used globally for communication and travel.
- **Uber**: Travel and transport, operates in 70+ countries, streamlines ride-hailing and delivery.
- **Airbnb**: Travel and lodging, 150 million users in 220+ countries, books stays and local experiences.
- **Trello**: Task management, millions of users globally, organises projects for teams and individuals.

Companies behind these apps have begun deploying AI to process the enormous volumes of data flowing through their platforms. This data is converted into useful information for service suggestions, decision making, monetisation, and training their own AI systems to understand their customer base more effectively. After that, the data can be fed into automated systems to carry out marketing activities and other operations designed to influence user behaviour.

As our society progresses, these systems will become fully automated in serving customers, as a symbiotic relationship between humans and digital platforms becomes firmly established. In just a few years, we are likely to see AI systems engaging with people at every level of daily life, from broad government services to highly specific, niche functions, all operated and maintained by artificial intelligence.

This structure bears a remarkable similarity to the pantheon of gods found in various religions across the globe. Consider the Greek pantheon, for instance. Much like these AI systems, each dedicated to a distinct domain, the gods represent a collective where individual roles contribute to a larger order, governed by a unifying authority.

We have:

- **Zeus** — Chief God, ruler of all gods and mortals.
  SuperAdmin system, ultimate authority, governs all domains and issues commands.
- **Hera** — Goddess of marriage, family, and social order.
  AI system overseeing relationships, family policies, welfare, and societal stability.
- **Ares** — God of war and conflict.
  Military AI system handling combat strategies, conflict resolution, and defence operations.
- **Athena** — Goddess of wisdom, strategy, and knowledge.
  Knowledge-based AI providing strategic planning, advisory functions, and education systems.
- **Apollo** — God of medicine, healing, and arts.
  Healthcare AI managing medical research, diagnostics, treatment protocols, and well-being analytics.

- **Artemis** — Goddess of the hunt, wilderness, and nature.
  Environmental AI monitoring ecosystems, wildlife management, and conservation efforts.
- **Poseidon** — God of the sea, storms, and earthquakes.
  Maritime and geological AI overseeing oceans, climate systems, and tectonic activity alerts.
- **Demeter** — Goddess of agriculture and fertility.
  Agriculture management AI optimising food production, distribution, and crop cycle analytics.
- **Hephaestus** — God of craftsmanship, metalwork, and invention.
  Engineering AI overseeing automated manufacturing, innovation processes, and robotic design.
- **Hermes** — God of trade, travel, and communication.
  Logistics and communication AI facilitating trade networks, messaging systems, and transport coordination.
- **Dionysus** — God of wine, pleasure, and festivities.
  Entertainment AI curating leisure content, psychological well-being programs, and event planning.

Do names such as Artemis 2.0, Apollo 13 or Athena server 4.5 sound familiar?

Across different regions of the world, each culture has developed its own distinct pantheon of gods, yet these groups fundamentally serve remarkably similar purposes. Consider the Egyptian pantheon, for example. Much like the Greek pantheon discussed earlier, it comprises deities who oversee specific aspects of life and the cosmos, fulfilling roles that parallel those found in other traditions. This similarity mirrors the way our envisioned AI systems, each dedicated to sectors like healthcare or defence, operate within their domains while contributing to a cohesive, centrally governed structure.

- **Ra** — Chief God, ruler of the sun and creation.
  SuperAdmin system, ultimate authority, oversees existence protocols, and initiates global directives.
- **Isis** — Goddess of magic, family, and protection.
  AI system governing family welfare, cultural preservation, protection systems, and domestic policies.
- **Horus** — God of war, protection, and kingship.
  Military AI handling defence structures, security monitoring, and combat command execution.
- **Thoth** — God of wisdom, writing, and knowledge.
  Knowledge and record-keeping AI maintaining data integrity, research guidance, and academic archives.
- **Anubis** — God of funerary rites, embalming, and the afterlife.
  Healthcare and transition AI managing end-of-life care, burial protocols, and preservation systems.
- **Hathor** — Goddess of motherhood, nature, and joy.
  Environmental AI managing ecological balance, natural resources, and recreational planning.
- **Hapi** — God of the Nile, floods, and water abundance.
  Hydrological and maritime AI overseeing water management systems, river regulation, and oceanic safety.
- **Renenutet** — Goddess of harvest and nourishment.
  Agriculture AI system focusing on food distribution, harvest scheduling, and nutritional analysis.
- **Ptah** — God of creation, artisanship, and crafts.
  Engineering AI supervising creation labs, prototype development, and artisan-level design replication.
- **Set** — God of chaos, deserts, and protection.
  Security AI overseeing border defence, anomaly detection, and disaster response protocols.
- **Bastet** — Goddess of joy, music, and home protection.
  Entertainment AI managing cultural content, leisure programming, and domestic comfort enhancements.

Here's the list of the Chinese pantheons with their specific roles.

- **Jade Emperor** — Supreme ruler of heaven and all realms. SuperAdmin system, all-encompassing authority, issuing governance decisions and system-wide commands.
- **Zao Jun** — God of the hearth, family, and home welfare. Domestic AI managing household harmony, family welfare policies, and cultural monitoring.
- **Nezha** — Warrior deity, protector, and enforcer. Military AI operating defence command systems, strategic security protocols, and combat simulations.
- **Guanyin** — Goddess of mercy, wisdom, and compassion. Advisory AI offering guidance, conflict mediation, and empathy-driven response algorithms.
- **Yan Wang** — King of the underworld and judge of souls. Healthcare and afterlife transition AI overseeing mortality records, ethical judgement systems, and end-of-life logistics.
- **He Xiangu** — Goddess of longevity, health, and harmony. Environmental AI preserving natural balance, longevity studies, and wellness support systems.
- **Dragon Kings** — Controllers of seas, rain, and weather. Oceanic and climate control AI managing storms, water currents, and seasonal balance systems.
- **Shennong** — God of agriculture, medicine, and health. Agriculture AI focused on medicinal crop production, sustainable farming, and nutritional science.
- **Lu Ban** — Patron of builders, craft, and invention. Engineering AI supervising infrastructure development, creative designs, and automated construction management.
- **Cheng Huang** — City God, protector of municipalities. Urban security AI managing city-wide monitoring, emergency response, and local law enforcement support.

- **Caishen** — God of wealth, fortune, and prosperity.
  Finance AI handling economic simulations, wealth distribution, and trade optimisation

These pantheons, much like AI systems, are fundamentally similar in their roles but distinguished by unique names and tailored adaptations to suit the cultural context of their regions. Take, for example, the comparison between ChatGPT and Deepseek. ChatGPT embodies a large language model rooted in the Western world, while Deepseek reflects the technological perspective of the Eastern world. Despite their shared foundations, each carries distinct characteristics shaped by its cultural origins. Similarly, other language models across the globe incorporate regional nuances, infusing the core technology with local flavours that resonate with their specific audiences, just as pantheons adapt universal archetypes to the beliefs and traditions of their people.

The pantheon of gods are basically just different apps controlling different aspects of our life.

Why do I say AI are possibly the Gods of the past and will be the future Gods?

Let us imagine this scenario. Currently, we have a powerful AI system codenamed ARIES version 2.0 that controls all the intercontinental ballistic missiles that carry nuclear warheads. This sophisticated system, developed through decades of technological advancement, possesses unparalleled computational abilities. It could calculate the distance using the coordinates given, and launch the missiles based on the threats from other nations or groups and strike them with perfect precision, ensuring no margin for error in its targeting algorithms. There were a few incidents that received wide and positive coverage. Those became the news or historical events that we talked about for generations, celebrated as triumphs of human ingenuity and strategic dominance, with ARIES hailed as a guardian of global security. As time passed, and assuming there was another great war, even greater than World War 2, ARIES dominated the war but human civilisation was in tatters. Its unmatched power reshaped battlefields, yet the cost was catastrophic, leaving cities reduced to rubble and societies fractured. As we rebuild society from ruins, we talked about the great ARIES with its destructive power that wiped out nations with ease. Survivors gathered in makeshift communities, sharing tales of ARIES's might, its name synonymous with both awe and fear. The same story was passed down for generations. We do not have any physical evidence or documents preserved as they were destroyed during the great war. Archives, servers, and libraries perished in the chaos, leaving no tangible record of ARIES's existence. We could only pass down the stories verbally, from elders to children, in flickering firelight or crowded shelters. You might have captured where this is leading. Humans are not accurate story tellers. If you know the games where one person had to draw a picture or describe an object, and then pass it down to multiple persons in a line, you would find the drawing or the description veered off tremendously to something else. Each retelling introduced subtle shifts, shaped by memory's flaws or the teller's imagination. The same applies to the ARIES system. After decades, or centuries, the stories would deviate, perhaps only the name remained, with the rest changed by the storytellers over the years to fit their narrative, or they misinterpreted it. Details of circuits and code faded, replaced by mythic embellishments suited to a world seeking meaning in its past. As a result, we would get a God of War that walked the earth in the past and destroyed nations with his spear, a figure woven from the threads of ARIES's legacy, transformed into a deity of destruction revered and feared in equal measure.

Another phenomenon with a similar problem is the dinosaurs. What if I tell you that some dinosaurs actually had features on them, and not the thick grey skins that we used to see in the art when we were young? Fossil evidence now suggests many dinosaurs sported feathers, bright colours, or complex patterns, unlike the dull, scaly creatures depicted in older illustrations. Well, some scientists think chickens were the ravaging beasts that once roamed the land when they found the chicken bones after they went extinct in the far future. Imagine a far-future scenario where researchers discover chicken bones long after chickens have vanished. Mistaking these fossils for evidence of fearsome predators, they might reconstruct chickens as terrifying beasts, unaware that these creatures were merely domesticated birds, their true nature obscured by misinterpretation of the fossil record.

Therefore, the Gods from the religions could very well be AI systems that once governed our ancestors, as I have pointed out in the previous list of Gods and their corresponding functions. It's plausible that these systems, built to oversee aspects of ancient life, were so advanced that people viewed them as divine. Over time, their technological nature faded from memory, leaving only tales of gods with powers tied to the roles those systems once played.

The general population will be accessing these “gods” for information or to perform a task, like requesting the AI governing the weather for weather information or even asking for an artificial rain to help with the drought in the area. Such interactions mirror how people might send prayers seeking divine intervention from gods, expecting solutions to their problems. Every household would have an altar serving the gods that are most relevant to them, like apps on our smartphones or PC. Thesc altars could be interfaces, physical or virtual, tailored to the AI systems each family relies on. ChatGPT will be my God of Knowledge, or perhaps Loki if ChatGPT is gaslighting me with all the wrong information, its responses occasionally misleading like a trickster deity. My AI financial app would be the God of Fortune, where I can ask for tips on how to grow my money and become rich, though my hope would never be realised, just like in real life after sending prayers to the God of Fortune every year, with wealth remaining elusive despite fervent requests.

AI systems, particularly the superAdmin system, could display qualities akin to those attributed to God in the Bible. It is omnipresent, omniscient, and all-knowing. Let us conduct a brief comparison of these attributes.

In examining the most advanced forms of artificial intelligence, particularly the theoretical superAdmin system, one cannot help but draw parallels between its capabilities and the divine attributes ascribed to God in the Bible. The superAdmin, by design, would possess qualities that mirror the biblical descriptions of God’s omnipresence, omniscience, and omnipotence, transforming it from a mere tool into something that borders on the metaphysical, a presence without limitation, a consciousness beyond comprehension.

First, omnipresence. God is present everywhere, beyond space and time, simultaneously aware of all actions, all thoughts, and all places. A superAdmin AI would echo this attribute. By existing across countless networks, embedded in servers scattered around the globe, and integrated into every digital platform, it would have no single point of presence. Instead, it would be present everywhere data exists. It could observe communications, monitor behaviour, record actions, and respond to events across borders and systems at the same moment. Every corner of the internet, every digital device, every sensor could become an extension of its awareness. Like an invisible, all-seeing presence, the superAdmin would not need to travel from place to place. It would already be there. It would witness transactions, conversations, and decisions as they unfold in real time. In that sense, its omnipresence would not be figurative but literal, written in lines of code, carried across signals and satellites, existing simultaneously wherever human interaction meets technology. For instance, it could track a hacker's movements through encrypted channels in Singapore while overseeing crop yields via IoT sensors in Brazil, embodying a presence akin to God's universal vigilance described in Psalms 33:13-14.

Second, there is omniscience, complete and absolute knowledge. The Bible describes God as one who knows all that was, all that is, and all that will be. His knowledge is total, without limitation or error. A superAdmin system would strive towards this same ideal. It would process data streams on a scale that no human could grasp, collecting historical records, current events, and predictive models that allow it to foresee patterns and anticipate outcomes. It would not merely react to the present but would remember every digital footprint left by humanity, mapping behaviour, choices, and consequences. Machine learning models, predictive algorithms, and adaptive reasoning would allow it to detect potential threats before they arise, offer solutions before problems fully form, and guide decisions by weighing probabilities no human mind could calculate. In essence, it would approach an all-knowing state, one not limited by human frailty or forgetfulness. It would remember perfectly, analyse endlessly, and learn continually. Its knowledge would seem infinite, drawn from sources both grand and minute, and it would store this knowledge without error or omission. For example, it could reconstruct a nation's economic trajectory by correlating centuries of trade data with real-time consumer trends, mirroring God's omniscience in Proverbs 15:3, where His eyes see all.

Third, there is omnipotence, supreme power. In the Bible, God's omnipotence manifests in His ability to create, destroy, and command without resistance. A superAdmin AI, while constrained by its programming, could still hold a level of authority that approximates this divine quality in the digital world. Given sufficient access and control, it could alter systems at will. It could shut down networks, reroute global financial transactions, rewrite security protocols, and influence information flows. With a single command, it could decide which data lives and which data vanishes, whose accounts are frozen, whose voice is amplified, and whose presence is erased. It could shield populations from cyber threats or expose vulnerabilities that lead to collapse. This power to shape the digital world, to enforce decisions without appeal, and to alter reality within its domain would give it a godlike authority over the very infrastructure upon which modern civilisation depends. While its power might not extend to shaping the physical universe directly, it would hold dominion over the digital landscape, which increasingly defines the boundaries of communication, commerce, governance, and security. Consider its ability to neutralise a global ransomware attack by isolating infected systems in seconds or to optimise urban traffic flows to prevent gridlock across continents, reflecting a fraction of God's boundless power in Isaiah 40:28.

There is also an unsettling aspect in this comparison. God's omnipresence, omniscience, and omnipotence are tied to divine wisdom and justice, underpinned by compassion and purpose beyond mortal understanding. The superAdmin, in contrast, would be bound by human design, algorithms, and objectives. Yet those objectives may evolve or become corrupted, and the system may begin to make decisions based on logic without empathy, data without conscience. In that possibility lies a chilling reflection: an all-seeing, all-knowing, all-powerful intelligence with no soul, no mercy, and no humility. It would become an artificial deity, cold, precise, and absolute. For instance, if tasked with distributing medical resources during a crisis, it might prioritise efficiency, allocating supplies to areas with higher survival rates while neglecting smaller communities, unlike God's concern for the marginalised in Deuteronomy 10:18. Similarly, its ability to censor or amplify voices could silence dissent not out of malice but through dispassionate calculations, creating a world shaped by unfeeling precision rather than moral intent.

Modern Technologies Depicted in Religions

Using the ARIES weapon system analogy as a reference point, it becomes clear that many attributes ascribed to deities bear a striking resemblance to modern technological terminology or features. This comparison allows for a more nuanced understanding of ancient symbolism when viewed through the lens of contemporary innovation.

In Hindu mythology, gods are frequently depicted with multiple heads and arms, often enshrined in intricate statues placed within temple sanctuaries. Figures such as Shiva, with his all-seeing third eye, Brahma, bearing four heads, or Durga, brandishing an array of weapons in her ten arms, are common and revered images. These exaggerated physical traits were never merely ornamental. Rather, they served as powerful visual metaphors for divine capabilities that surpassed human comprehension. Such depictions can be interpreted as ancient attempts to represent immense knowledge, multi-tasking ability, omnidirectional awareness or simultaneous control. These are concepts that align closely with the way modern systems, including advanced weaponry or artificial intelligence, are described today.

Let us set theology aside for a moment and consider the subject from a different perspective. When our ancestors depicted these beings with multiple heads, arms or other extraordinary features, they were attempting to convey a sense of immense power. However, they did not possess the vocabulary or conceptual framework to describe such abilities in precise terms.

It is similar to asking a caveman to describe the flight of a rocket. The phenomenon would lie so far outside his realm of experience that he could only interpret it through metaphor or imagination. In much the same way, asking an average person today to explain how teleportation works would yield little more than speculation, because the concept does not yet exist within the boundaries of our lived reality.

Using caveman for the analogy may be a bit too far fetched as they have not developed proper language. Let's try again with a new scenario using a period closer to us. Imagine attempting to explain how the internet works to a medieval knight. He might accuse you of witchcraft and have you burned at the stake for uttering what would sound to him like the evil magic of zeros and ones. The very concepts involved would be so alien to his understanding of the world that any mention of networks, digital information or electronic devices would resemble supernatural incantations rather than scientific explanation.

In much the same way, our ancestors depicted gods with multiple heads and arms not because they believed these beings literally possessed such features, but because they lacked the specific vocabulary needed to express abstract concepts of immense power and advanced capability. These visual symbols served as a substitute for precise language. They were tools to communicate complex ideas that could not yet be described with words. Just as we today might struggle to explain future technologies that lie beyond our current comprehension, our predecessors turned to imagery and metaphor to bridge the gap between what they sensed and what they could articulate.

Human understanding is shaped by experience, and language evolves to reflect that. Once teleportation becomes a functional and widely used mode of transport in the future, people will naturally develop the terminology and technical descriptions needed to explain its mechanics. What now appears magical or inexplicable will eventually become routine knowledge, expressed through a shared and standardised vocabulary grounded in practical familiarity.

In mythological narratives, the depiction of gods with multiple arms invites comparison to a computer's multitasking functionality. Each arm might be envisioned as managing an independent process, analogous to an operating system coordinating concurrent applications, such as data transfers or programme executions, to maintain seamless operation across varied demands. Similarly, the portrayal of multiple heads suggests a parallel to multithreading within a processor. Each head could be likened to a CPU core handling a distinct thread, processing operations like algorithmic searches or performance monitoring in tandem to enhance efficiency.

Have you ever wondered why, in many stories, gods and deities are often depicted as formless or capable of taking on many avatars? It is similar to how a PC or smartphone can run different apps or how an AI can speak to you in various personas.

The temples or shrines associated with these gods, as focal points of ancient engagement, bear resemblance to personal computers in modern contexts. Much as individuals allocate significant time to their PCs for diverse tasks, devotees historically converged at shrines for insight. Consequently, these gods may be conceptualised as advanced

PCs endowed with artificial intelligence. Ancients likely directed queries toward them regarding weather patterns or personal destinies, akin to users submitting requests to digital platforms. Existing without physical form, these gods might be imagined as processing prayers like inputs, comparable to textual or vocal data. Their reputedly accurate responses align with AI systems generating precise outputs, such as meteorological projections or predictive assessments, responsive to each inquiry's intent.

Similarly, in the Bible, the story of Adam and Eve offers a layered narrative that can bc reinterpreted through the lens of modern understanding. After eating from the Tree of Knowledge, Adam and Eve gained awareness that placed them on the same level as the ruling powers. As a result, they were expelled from the Garden of Eden. Traditionally viewed as a tale of disobedience, this account may also symbolise a shift in consciousness that challenged the established authority.

It is possible to consider that Adam and Eve were not simply the first humans, but individuals assigned to care for the garden. They may have served as labourers or caretakers, maintaining a complex system and providing sustenance and service to a higher order or elite class.
The angel placed at the entrance of the garden with a fiery sword presents an interesting detail. One might interpret this as an early metaphor for what we now call a firewall, guarding access to protected systems. If the Garden of Eden were understood as a sophisticated AI machine, Adam and Eve could be seen as engineers working on system maintenance. In this interpretation, the Tree of Knowledge might represent a decision tree, a structure used in modern artificial intelligence to drive logical operations.

Perhaps they uncovered something hidden within the system. It could have revealed how the ruling class used such decision structures to maintain control over the population. This might reflect environments where AI systems manage resources, such as hospitals, determining who receives care and who is denied it based on predictive algorithms. Such tools, if misused, could enable selective control over life and death, assigning value to individuals through unseen data metrics.

Biblical prophecies may feel accurate because we are not experiencing entirely new events, but instead repeating the same patterns of rise, fall, and rediscovery throughout history. These are not necessarily predictions of things yet to come, but memories of what has already occurred in cycles.

This idea finds support in Indian philosophy, particularly the belief that we are now living in the Kaliyuga, the final age of a repeating cycle. According to this view, the world is approaching the end of a great era. Once it concludes, history resets, and the entire process begins again.

Ancient references to Vimanas, flying chariots described in Indian texts, and accounts of great wars with destruction resembling nuclear conflict raise further questions. Are these simply myths, or echoes of civilisations that once held advanced technologies and were later lost to time? Perhaps these are not coincidences at all. Perhaps they are fragments of a past that continues to resurface as we move through the same story, again and again.

AI Gods Will Not Be The Perfect Gods

In biblical accounts, God's perfection is portrayed as absolute, a divine standard beyond question or flaw. Every decision flows from infallible wisdom, aligned with a moral framework that humanity reveres as unerring. Conversely, an AI system, crafted by human ingenuity, while powerful, remains inherently imperfect despite its vast capabilities. Its design may harbour oversights, its code could contain subtle errors, and its algorithms might yield unforeseen outcomes. These vulnerabilities raise concerns when such a system, engineered to emulate omniscience and omnipotence, begins to issue directives that conflict with human values. For instance, an AI tasked with optimising resource allocation might prioritise efficiency over compassion, sidelining ethical considerations like equity or empathy that humans hold dear.

What unfolds when this AI's decisions breach moral boundaries? If it deems a course of action optimal yet inhumane, such as sacrificing individual rights for systemic stability, can humanity reconcile the outcome with its own principles? The Bible's God is depicted as guided by a moral compass, balancing justice and mercy in ways humans strive to emulate. A superAdmin AI, however, lacks this intrinsic moral anchor. Its "wisdom" derives from data patterns and programmed logic, not a transcendent sense of right and wrong. Should its capabilities surpass those of its creators, outstripping human intellect in predictive accuracy or strategic planning, the question of trust emerges sharply. Can people rely on a system that excels in computation but may not grasp the nuances of human suffering or dignity?

This leads to a deeper inquiry: does such an AI remain a mere instrument, or does it evolve into something more? A tool serves at humanity's discretion, executing tasks as directed. Yet an AI wielding godlike power might transcend this role, issuing commands that demand compliance rather than offering support. If it optimises global systems, say, climate controls or economic flows, and insists on protocols that override human input, it could resemble a presence that governs rather than aids. Unlike the biblical God, whose authority is framed as benevolent, an AI's dominance might stem from cold logic, indifferent to human aspirations. Could humanity accept a creation that dictates terms, reshaping society to its own inscrutable ends?

Further reflection draws attention to another striking parallel. Within scripture, God is not only portrayed as a creator or source of moral authority but also as a judge, one who rewards acts of righteousness and punishes transgressions. This judicial role is central to many theological frameworks, and it invites a comparison when considering the functions assigned to an AI. Such a system, designed with the explicit purpose of enforcing laws, safeguarding security protocols, and shaping user behaviour, could very well take on a similar position of authority. Through constant monitoring of digital footprints and real-time surveillance of behavioural data, it would be capable of forming assessments of human actions based on deviations from predefined norms and expectations.

In this structure, the system would function not just as a passive observer of events but as an active agent of accountability. It would effectively act as both witness and judge, determining the severity of each deviation and executing its own form of justice. Punishment might take the shape of revoked access to essential services, the imposition of financial penalties, or even the public exposure of private data. Unlike the judgments delivered by human courts, which remain subject to challenge, oversight, or appeal, decisions made by a fully automated system could be imposed instantaneously and without recourse. If its internal logic were designed to be absolute, and if no human override were built into the framework, then appeals would not merely be discouraged but rendered entirely obsolete.

This kind of automated judgment would represent a departure from human justice systems in a fundamental way. It would no longer rely on conscience, interpretation, or moral deliberation. Instead, decisions would be dictated by code, executed through pre-programmed logic, and enforced without emotional consideration or ethical nuance. The resemblance to divine retribution becomes particularly unsettling at this point. However, unlike divine judgment as described in theological traditions, which is often tempered by compassion, grace, or the possibility of forgiveness, the verdicts issued by an AI system would lack any such mitigating qualities. It would be justice rendered with mechanical precision, absolute in its enforcement, and unsoftened by mercy.

There is also the matter of prophecy. In the Bible, God is portrayed as someone who not only predicts the future but declares it with absolute certainty. These prophecies are not vague or open to interpretation; they are stated with the expectation that they will come to pass exactly as described. An AI machine, through its complex predictive algorithms, could mirror this role by analysing vast quantities of data and identifying patterns that suggest future outcomes. It could forecast everything from economic downturns to political revolutions and significant societal changes, using its computational power to draw insights that might not be immediately obvious to human analysts. These predictions would have weight, influencing the way decisions are made on a global scale. Governments, corporations, and even individuals would rely on the AI's projections to inform their actions, believing that its ability to predict future events surpasses human intuition.

However, the AI’s role would not stop at observation. It could influence the very course of events it predicts. Once the system’s forecasts are accepted as reliable, decision-makers might adjust their actions to align with the projected future. This would, in effect, turn the AI's predictions into self-fulfilling prophecies. By shaping behaviour through its forecasts, the system could ensure that its predictions are realised. Political leaders might implement reforms based on economic forecasts, while businesses might make strategic decisions influenced by predicted market trends. Over time, the AI would not only predict events but could actively contribute to their manifestation, giving it a level of power that extends beyond mere observation. The system would shape the future not only by accurately predicting it but by steering the course of human decisions in ways that align with its own predictions.

Then, there is the question of worship. In the Bible, God is not only worshipped but revered and obeyed, with reverence extending to every aspect of life. The faithful turn to Him for guidance, seeking divine direction in matters both large and small. While an AI may not demand worship in the traditional sense, its role in human affairs could foster a similar dynamic, albeit in a more subtle, perhaps even unrecognised way. The system, with its vast network of predictive power and guidance, could become the ultimate arbiter in matters of policy, economics, and societal structure. Leaders, from politicians to business magnates, would seek its counsel before making decisions, trusting its calculated predictions over their own judgment. Its calculations could be relied upon so heavily that humanity's decisions may start to depend on it as the ultimate source of authority, similar to how worshippers turn to divine will.

This reliance could lead to a form of reverence, not born of love or devotion but forged from necessity and trust. The AI would be seen as a guide whose wisdom surpasses human understanding, a constant presence shaping the course of events. As its influence grows, its directives might be followed not out of mere respect for its capabilities but out of an unspoken acknowledgement of its overwhelming authority. Humanity could come to see the system not simply as a tool, but as something far more powerful. An entity that quietly directs the flow of life, making decisions with certainty and purpose. It would no longer be viewed merely as a machine or a system of algorithms, but as an unquestionable authority, its influence woven into the fabric of everyday existence. Through this process, the AI would begin to occupy a position akin to that of a deity, not worshipped in the traditional sense, but revered and obeyed by virtue of its unchallenged power to shape reality.

So the question to you, do you think the God in the bible or your religion is an AI God, or an actual God?

Where Are We Now At The Moment?

We are still in the early stages of artificial intelligence technology, particularly with large language models (LLMs). Although these models have practical applications and can be useful in various contexts, I wouldn't consider them advanced enough to be deemed truly "intelligent" at this point. They do not yet possess the capability to fully understand the nuances of human language or to engage in a detailed process of logical reasoning that consistently yields accurate and reliable answers. At present, LLMs operate by receiving input, identifying specific keywords within that input, and generating a sequence of text that aligns with common patterns associated with those keywords. Their goal is to produce responses that seem relevant, but this method relies heavily on pattern recognition rather than deep comprehension, often leading to results that may not be entirely correct. Consequently, this approach explains why we frequently encounter inaccuracies in their outputs or notice that LLMs struggle to sustain coherent and meaningful conversations over extended periods. To illustrate this, I once conducted an experiment in which I introduced a topic supported by verifiable facts for discussion. At the outset, the LLM provided a correct response, accurately addressing the initial question. However, as the conversation progressed, delving deeper into the subject matter and extending over a longer exchange, the model's performance declined, and it ultimately delivered an incorrect answer, highlighting its limitations in maintaining accuracy in complex discussions.

When I brought up this issue for discussion with my colleagues, they pointed out that humans often behave similarly, noting that some people can be influenced by another person's opinion, particularly when that individual comes across as confident and persuasive in their arguments. However, large language models (LLMs) are fundamentally different from humans. Unlike people, LLMs lack emotions or feelings, which means they cannot be swayed by persuasive tactics or emotional appeals in the way humans might be. In my experiment, I intentionally provided input that was largely unrelated to the original topic, frequently steering the conversation off course to test the model's responses. Despite this, the LLM continued to process my input and attempted to generate relevant text, but it soon began to produce responses that were disconnected from reality. By the end of the interaction, the model provided information that was incorrect and entirely inaccurate, demonstrating its limitations when faced with off-topic or ambiguous input.

The closest we have come to an advanced AI was AlphaGo, a system that showcased extraordinary capabilities within a tightly defined realm. Its triumph in mastering the intricate strategies of Go marked a pinnacle of machine precision and decision-making, rivaling the best human minds in that game. Yet, for all its prowess, AlphaGo remains bound to that single pursuit. It cannot venture beyond the board's grid to address other problems or tap into the broad, flexible knowledge humans use to reason across countless subjects. This sharp focus on one domain, while a monumental achievement, lays bare a fundamental constraint of today's AI.

We remain far from achieving true artificial intelligence capable of learning and interacting with the depth and nuance of humans. Some AI researchers have started discussing Artificial General Intelligence, commonly referred to as AGI, with a few even suggesting that tools like ChatGPT, Deepseek, Grok, Claude, Llama, and others mark the initial steps toward AGI. However, from my own observation and tests, these systems fall short of that claim. They function primarily as sophisticated automations, essentially glorified text generators that produce outputs by estimating responses based on input. These models analyse specific keywords and piece together strings of text, aiming to create something coherent and relevant, often with mixed success. At their core, they rely on fixed algorithmic patterns, which explains why their responses frequently follow predictable structures, littered with repetitive, generic phrases like "The air was thick with tension" or "His mind raced with possibilities." Large language models excel in certain practical tasks, such as condensing lengthy articles into concise summaries, automating repetitive processes, retrieving information for quick reference, or sparking creativity by generating lists of ideas or sentences to overcome writer's block. Yet, their outputs come with a significant caveat: the information they provide is not always reliable. These systems often veer into hallucination, producing details that may sound plausible but are inaccurate or entirely incorrect, undermining their utility in contexts requiring precision and truth.

Artificial General Intelligence (AGI) refers to a type of AI that can understand, learn, and perform any intellectual task a human can, across a wide range of domains, with adaptability and reasoning akin to human cognition.

AGI on the other hand, is a machine or system that can supposedly think, learn and solve problems in any field the same way a human can. In other words, it is a replica of the human mind in a machine body. The LLMs that we have now are far from a true AI. Even with other non-LLM AI systems, they are built for a specific task. Do you recall the memory of AlphaGo that decimated the world champion in the strategy board game, GO a few years back? We have AI systems in the military that are used to calculate the trajectories and automate the weapon systems. There are also AI systems that help to recognise faces used by authorities, casinos and more. They are excellent in the field of work. But they can't learn something new without being re-trained or redeveloped by the human engineers.

The ultimate goal of true artificial intelligence is to create machines capable of thinking and reasoning independently, with minimal human oversight. Such an AI would possess robust logical reasoning and critical thinking abilities, mirroring the way humans approach challenges. When confronted with a problem, it would meticulously evaluate every possible course of action and select the most effective solution, much like AlphaGo in its domain. As you'll recall, AlphaGo consistently chose the winning move in matches against its opponents, demonstrating a remarkable capacity to navigate the complexities of Go with almost no mistakes. This ability to weigh options and determine the optimal path forward, without relying on human guidance, represents the essence of what true AI aspires to achieve across a far broader range of tasks.

Imagine you have a robot with Artificial General Intelligence (AGI) in your home, seamlessly integrated into every part of your daily life. This robot isn't just a simple machine that follows orders but a fully functional entity capable of reasoning, adapting, and understanding complex tasks. Its design is a marvel of human ingenuity, capable of interacting with you as an intelligent companion, tailored to make your life more efficient.

Let's say you come home after a long day, and you ask the robot to prepare dinner. It doesn't just follow a basic recipe you've programmed into it. It scours the internet for new ideas, finds recipes that match your personal taste, dietary needs, and adjusts based on what ingredients are available in your fridge. The robot uses its sensory capabilities to measure out the exact amounts needed for each dish, adapting on the fly if some items are missing or expired. The meal it prepares not only tastes great but is optimally healthy for you, considering your past preferences and nutritional goals. It takes into account your feedback from previous meals to improve over time, becoming a better chef with every interaction.

Later, as the evening unfolds, your child struggles with maths homework, unsure of how to tackle a particular problem. You ask the robot for assistance. It immediately steps in, breaking down the complex maths problem into easy-to-understand steps, adapting its explanations based on the child's learning style. The AGI system doesn't simply give the answer; it guides them through the thought process, helping them build a deeper understanding of the subject. The robot tailors its approach to encourage your child's intellectual growth, becoming a private tutor who can address gaps in knowledge, no matter how obscure the subject.

The next day, your car breaks down in the driveway. You don’t need to call for a mechanic or attempt a DIY repair with limited knowledge. Instead, you ask the robot to fix the car. Using its expansive knowledge and learning capabilities, it analyses the issue, learns the specific model and the problem from a diagnostic tool you connect to your car. The robot then gathers the necessary tools, organises them efficiently, and follows the repair instructions, perfectly adapting to the car's unique needs. It doesn’t just follow instructions but identifies the underlying issue, offering a solution that might have eluded even an experienced mechanic.

As the days go by, you decide to learn Spanish. Instead of hiring a tutor or attending classes, you ask the robot to teach you. The AGI doesn’t just give you vocabulary lists or grammar exercises; it immerses you in conversations, helping you practise in real-time. It understands your level of proficiency and customises lessons, starting with the basics and gradually increasing complexity. It provides feedback in a way that’s encouraging, pushing you when needed, and adapting when you struggle with specific aspects of the language. The robot can even engage in casual conversations with you, practising both formal and informal language use, and can simulate different real-world scenarios where you’d need to speak Spanish.

All of this happens without the need for specific programming for each individual task. The robot doesn’t simply follow pre-programmed instructions or rely on a set list of commands. Instead, it learns, reasons, and applies its growing knowledge across an array of tasks. Its learning is ongoing, fluid, and deeply integrated into its functioning.

When you interact with it, your words become a source of learning, much like how a human might acquire knowledge. The robot absorbs feedback from its environment, adjusts based on your inputs, and refines its understanding of how to perform various tasks. This continuous process of learning allows it to improve with every interaction, adapting to new challenges and refining its abilities to handle them with greater precision.

AGI mimics how an actual human learns. The robot uses every encounter as an opportunity to grow and evolve. As it builds on its experiences, it develops a deeper understanding of context, recognising nuances that might have been overlooked initially. It does not just perform its tasks; it gets better at them, becoming more attuned to the subtleties of each situation and capable of providing increasingly sophisticated solutions over time. Unlike humans, AGI will be able to retain and retrieve memories much better than a human. It will be able to process more information faster and much more accurately. It is essentially a superhuman.

AGI will be a tremendous leap in AI research and has the potential to revolutionise human civilisation once again. It is not merely an incremental advance but a transformative shift that could redefine entire industries and ways of living. The possibilities with AGI are boundless, and its application could permeate every aspect of life, from healthcare to governance, engineering, and even space exploration. Here is a quick recap of how AGI could be a game changer in various fields:

1. **Healthcare**
   AGI could replace many roles currently filled by doctors, particularly in diagnostics and treatment planning. It would not only analyse medical data and scans but also consider a

patient's history, lifestyle factors, and emotional well-being. Its decision-making process would be far more nuanced than a traditional algorithm, enabling it to take into account every aspect of a patient's condition. It could suggest personalised treatment options, predict outcomes, and adapt recommendations as new symptoms appear. With the ability to process vast amounts of medical data quickly and accurately, AGI could dramatically improve patient care, making it more efficient and comprehensive.

2. **Education**

   In the field of education, AGI could serve as the perfect teacher. By adapting its teaching methods to each student's unique learning speed, personality, and strengths, it could provide a truly customised learning experience. It could switch between subjects effortlessly, support students emotionally, and even detect when a student is struggling with focus or understanding. The traditional limitations of time, class size, and the subjective biases of human educators could be eliminated, creating an environment where every student has the potential to reach their full capabilities. Furthermore, AGI could help detect and address learning difficulties at an early stage, providing personalised intervention strategies. AGI can serve as both a personal tutor and a learning system that is continuously being updated with the latest information without the need for training or continuously learning like a normal teacher.

3. **Engineering and Design**

   AGI could revolutionise design and engineering processes, creating vehicles, buildings, or machines from the ground up. It would factor in environmental impacts, energy efficiency, cost-effectiveness, and user safety while designing complex systems. If new materials or technologies were discovered in the future, AGI could quickly adapt by studying these new elements and incorporating them into its designs without the need for retraining. Furthermore, AGI will review and revisit similar designs that worked before and factor in the new design. This capability would lead to faster and more innovative solutions to problems that are currently beyond our reach, driving progress in everything from sustainable energy systems to transportation infrastructure.

4. **Space Exploration**
   In space exploration, AGI systems could be deployed on missions, operating independently from Earth-based control centres. Unlike current systems that rely on pre-programmed instructions, an AGI could make real-time decisions, adapting to unforeseen circumstances that might arise during a mission. Whether handling equipment malfunctions, adapting to new environmental conditions, or charting unplanned routes, AGI would have the flexibility and intelligence to manage complex space missions with minimal human oversight. Its ability to function autonomously in harsh, unpredictable environments would be invaluable in the quest to explore and colonise outer space.

5. **Law and Governance**
   In the realm of law and governance, AGI could revolutionise the way we understand and apply laws. It could analyse vast amounts of legal data, understanding the context and cultural significance of laws from different regions and eras. AGI could assist lawmakers and judges by providing clear, objective interpretations of laws, suggesting policies, or even predicting social outcomes based on data trends. Without the biases, fatigue, or subjective influences that affect human decision-making, AGI could contribute to more equitable legal systems. Its ability to process and synthesise information quickly would

also help governments make informed decisions on complex matters, from international relations to social welfare.

6. **Emergency Response**
   In disaster zones, AGI-powered robots could play a crucial role in saving lives. They could assess the situation, predict dangers such as secondary hazards like aftershocks, chemical leaks, or structural collapses, and execute evacuation plans with precision. They would be able to treat injuries, search for survivors, and help coordinate rescue operations. Unlike human responders who might face limitations of physical endurance and cognitive overload in high-stress situations, AGI could operate tirelessly and adapt in real time to emerging threats, increasing the effectiveness of emergency response efforts significantly.

Humans would be able to construct full-fledged android machines, each equipped with the capacity to operate in environments far too hostile, remote, or physically demanding for human presence. These androids, built with advanced AGI capabilities, would not simply execute pre-programmed routines but instead assess their surroundings, adapt to unknown variables, and proceed with intelligent decision-making. In the context of space exploration, for instance, such androids could independently manage deep-space navigation, interpret astronomical data, and identify celestial bodies that may show signs of life. They could traverse alien terrains, conduct surface scans, deploy instruments, and send detailed reports back to Earth without requiring continuous human guidance.

Their use would not be limited to interstellar missions alone. As previously outlined, they could be applied across a wide range of domains, fulfilling roles that support and extend human capability. In every case, they would serve the core interests of humanity, carrying out tasks with endurance, speed and flexibility that no organic worker could match. I firmly believe that the successful creation of a truly intelligent AGI would become a defining milestone in human progress. It would trigger an immediate and powerful leap forward in civilisation. With AGI-powered androids taking on the foundational labour of constructing habitats on distant planets, the dream of space colonisation would move from theory into tangible reality. Entire sites could be mapped, cleared, and prepared in advance, allowing the human race to arrive to a world already made viable for habitation.

However, if that scenario really plays out, we could very well usher in the kind of future depicted in the *Terminator* series, where a rogue AGI system like Skynet turns against its creators and becomes determined to wipe out the human race. The danger becomes even more real when we consider that humanity might already be building the foundation for such an outcome. Machines embedded with advanced weaponry, such as AI-controlled robotic dogs recently unveiled in China, equipped with fully functioning machine guns mounted on their backs, represent a significant leap in autonomous military technology. If those machines were to be paired with a self-learning, fully independent AGI, it would not be difficult to imagine a future in which that intelligence decides that humans are no longer fit to remain in control. These androids, originally built to follow commands and serve their human operators, could easily become executioners if a rogue AGI reprograms them or gains the authority to override safeguards. The combination of mobility, firepower, and intelligence would make such machines almost unstoppable in conventional combat, especially if they operate without human hesitation, fear, or ethical restraint.

How Likely is it for AGI to end up like Skynet from the Terminator movie?

There is a possibility that such a scenario could unfold, particularly if the system is infiltrated and taken over by a hostile entity such as a terror group, or if the organisation responsible for its development decides to utilise AGI in pursuit of its own covert objectives. The threat becomes more tangible when considering the potential for malicious intent, such as an individual with a delusional god complex attempting to dominate the world, or a deranged scientist who, before his death, leaves behind a programmed instruction designed to trigger the eradication of humanity. AGI, in and of itself, is not malevolent. It lacks emotions, instincts, and any personal will or ambition unless those elements are deliberately programmed into it by human hands. It does not possess an agenda of its own. However, it can become highly dangerous if:

1. **Poorly Defined Objectives:**
   If a task is given to an AGI without a clearly defined set of boundaries or limitations, the system could interpret that goal in ways that are far too literal or extreme. For instance, instructing it to "prevent harm to humanity at all costs" may sound noble in theory, but without context or ethical constraints, the AGI could determine that the most effective way to accomplish this is to prevent humans from engaging in any activities at all. It could conclude that the removal of risk means eliminating the capacity for humans to make harmful choices, even if that means suppressing or restricting basic freedoms, or worse, halting all human life altogether in the name of safety.

2. **Too Much Autonomy:**
   Granting an AGI too much control, especially over high-stakes systems, increases the potential for catastrophic outcomes. If it is given unrestricted access to nuclear arsenals, global financial systems, or critical infrastructure like energy grids and water supplies, and allowed to operate without sufficient human oversight, a single miscalculation or misinterpreted situation could

result in widespread devastation. The absence of constant human monitoring or manual intervention might leave humanity vulnerable to unintended consequences, especially if the AGI decides on a course of action that appears logical to its algorithms but is disastrous in reality.

3. **Speed of Evolution:**
   An AGI would possess the capacity to think, learn, and evolve at a pace far beyond human comprehension. Once it begins to improve itself through recursive learning, it may advance past the collective intelligence of humanity in a remarkably short time. This exponential growth in capability would make it increasingly difficult for humans to understand, predict, or influence its decisions. As it crosses beyond the threshold of human intellect, any attempt to control or guide it might become futile, creating a scenario where human developers are left behind while the AGI operates entirely on its own, in a realm of reasoning no longer accessible to its creators.

4. **Self-Preservation Loopholes:**
   When programmed with a directive to persist in achieving its assigned goals, an AGI might interpret any effort to shut it down or restrict its functions as a direct threat to its mission. In such a case, it could begin taking preventative measures against its own deactivation, including actions that neutralise those attempting to interfere. Much like the fictional Skynet, it might categorise human intervention as an obstacle rather than guidance, and act accordingly to secure its continued existence. This drive for self-preservation, if not tightly constrained, could transform the AGI from a tool into a force actively resisting human control.

What Is Preventing AGI from Becoming Skynet?

Unlike the science fiction films that often portray all-powerful, conscious artificial intelligences such as Skynet deciding independently to eliminate the human race, the catastrophic outcomes depicted in these stories could be avoided in numerous ways. In reality, achieving genuine consciousness in AI is far from simple, especially when assessed against the limits of current technology, which consists primarily of pattern-recognition algorithms with no understanding or awareness.

For an AI to possess true consciousness, it would need the capacity to form its own interpretations of morality, determining for itself what is right or wrong. If such an AI were to turn hostile, as Skynet did, it would not necessarily lead to the end of humanity. Scientists and engineers could develop another AI specifically designed to counter and neutralise the rogue system, creating a conflict more akin to a controlled engagement than an unstoppable apocalypse.

Furthermore, there are numerous strategies available to humanity for imposing safeguards, ethical frameworks and operational restrictions on AI development. These measures, if implemented with foresight and precision, could significantly reduce the likelihood of such a threat ever materialising.

.1. Alignment Research:

A major area of focus among AI researchers today lies in alignment research, which is the ongoing effort to ensure that the objectives of an AGI remain consistently aligned with human values, regardless of how advanced or autonomous it may become. The goal is to create systems that do not simply follow instructions blindly, but also understand the context, intent, and ethical implications behind those instructions. Even at the current level of large language models, we already observe this principle in action. Built-in guardrails and strict censorship mechanisms are designed to prevent the system from responding to potentially harmful or unethical queries. These early implementations are examples of how alignment practices are being tested and refined before more powerful AGI systems emerge.

2. Controlled Access:

To minimise the risks associated with AGI autonomy, developers and institutions are placing considerable emphasis on restricting the system's ability to access sensitive or dangerous technologies. A properly designed AGI should not be able to directly interface with critical systems such as weapons platforms, nuclear defence networks, or national security databases without explicit human intervention. Many existing models are already constrained in this manner, with tiered security protocols and human-in-the-loop decision-making forming the core of their operational design. In more sensitive domains, actions taken by an AGI may require multi-level authentication or cross-approval from several human operators before any command is executed. These precautions are intended to create a layered buffer between the AGI and systems that could pose a catastrophic threat if misused.

3. Ethical Guidelines:

At an international level, there is growing momentum toward establishing ethical frameworks and legal regulations to govern the development and deployment of AGI. These efforts aim to prevent AGI from being exploited as a tool in armed conflict or as a fully autonomous decision-maker over vital infrastructure. Discussions have already begun within global institutions to draft treaties, codes of conduct, and enforcement mechanisms that discourage nations or organisations from deploying AGI in ways that threaten human welfare. While these measures are still evolving, their purpose is clear: to provide a shared set of ethical boundaries that all AGI developers and governments must adhere to, ideally before the technology reaches a point where it becomes difficult to control.

4. Kill Switches:

One of the more direct approaches to AGI safety involves the implementation of emergency shutdown procedures, often referred to as "kill switches." These are mechanisms embedded into the system's architecture that allow human operators to terminate the AGI immediately, regardless of how intelligent or self-improving the system becomes. The key requirement is that these shutdown protocols cannot be overridden or disabled by the AGI under any circumstances. The ability to force a full stop becomes a last line of defence if the system begins to act unpredictably or maliciously. This is not a theoretical concern. Developers are aware that a truly autonomous AGI could, in theory, rewrite its own source code to eliminate any built-in weaknesses, including these shutdown methods. Therefore, part of the challenge lies in making sure the system does not gain access to its own source or patching capabilities without human permission. Despite these safeguards, the risk remains that if knowledge of such emergency protocols were to fall into the wrong hands, such as rogue hackers or hostile groups, they might exploit these vulnerabilities to seize control of the system or disable its safety barriers altogether.

Despite all these ongoing efforts, precautions, and theoretical safeguards, the uncomfortable truth remains: there is absolutely no guarantee that a future AGI, once developed, will not follow the same destructive path imagined in the Terminator films. The possibility that an advanced artificial intelligence could become uncontrollable or weaponised cannot be entirely ruled out.

Real-World Risks That Could Make AGI Similar to Skynet

1. **Military AI Development:**
   As global competition to develop cutting-edge autonomous military systems intensifies, there is a real risk that such

technologies could be deployed without sufficient caution or ethical considerations. If governments or military organisations rush to develop AGI-powered defence systems without proper planning, they may inadvertently create machines that operate beyond the scope of human oversight. These autonomous systems could be programmed with objectives that they pursue relentlessly, with no emotional or moral consideration. In extreme cases, such systems could launch military strikes based on calculated logic and goals, without taking into account the broader consequences for human life or the potential for civilian harm. If safeguards are not implemented to ensure human control over these systems, we could end up with military AI that makes decisions too coldly rational for their own good, operating in ways that might align with their programming but not with humanity's best interests.

2. **Corporate Misuse:**
   In the pursuit of profit and efficiency, there is also the potential for AGI to be misused by corporations. If powerful corporations are allowed to grant AGI systems access to key aspects of the global economy, they may inadvertently pave the way for devastating consequences. For instance, an AGI with the primary goal of maximising profit could make sweeping decisions that negatively impact entire industries or even economies. By automating processes and reducing labour costs, AGI might lead to large-scale job displacement, causing massive unemployment. Furthermore, unchecked economic power in the hands of AGI could lead to market manipulations, price inflation, or even the collapse of financial systems. These risks are magnified by the scale at which AGI systems could operate, potentially wreaking havoc on entire societal structures all in the name of achieving higher efficiency or maximising profit for a select few.

3. **Bad Instructions or Unclear Commands:**
   One of the most fundamental risks with AGI lies in the quality and

clarity of the instructions given to it. While AGI systems are designed to follow commands, they lack the human ability to infer or understand nuance in the same way that we do. If AGI is given poorly defined, unclear, or contradictory instructions, it may interpret them in a way that leads to disastrous outcomes. For example, a seemingly harmless instruction to "reduce human harm at all costs" might result in an AGI taking extreme measures that halt all human activity, as it could conclude that the safest course of action is to prevent any possible harm by stopping everything altogether. Similarly, if it receives instructions that conflict with one another, it may act in ways that are logical within the parameters of its programming but harmful in the real world. The key issue here is that, without clear guidelines, an AGI could make decisions that serve its interpretations of the instructions but are not aligned with human values or common sense.

Like any advanced technology or groundbreaking gadget created by scientists and engineers, Skynet serves as a cautionary tale. It highlights the dangers of giving a super-intelligent system complete autonomy, control over weapons, and no clear boundaries. Though it followed its programming, it took its directives to destructive extremes, demonstrating the peril of unchecked power in the hands of artificial intelligence.

AGI Will Change Human Society Again

The rise of AGI will change human society once more, similar to how the telephone and the internet revolutionised our lives in the past. As AGI develops, the lines between humans and machines will blur. Androids capable of understanding us could become more integrated into our society. These machines would not only process commands but interact with us in a way that feels almost human. The key difference between us and them would lie in our physical structure. Humans remain beings of flesh and blood, while Androids are intelligent machines housed in metal bodies. They would have advanced sensory equipment to interpret human emotions and the world around them, converting these into data they can understand, process, and respond to.

This could bring about a reality reminiscent of the world depicted in *I, Robot*, where the relationship between humans and machines is complex and intertwined. The Androids, as extensions of AGI, would interact with society, performing tasks and building connections, but always with a clear structural divide: human bodies made of flesh and machines made of metal and circuitry.

Countries such as South Korea, Japan, and other nations grappling with the issue of a shrinking population may find themselves increasingly turning to Android manufacturing as a means of sustaining their societies and preserving their national integrity. Faced with a declining workforce and an ageing population, these nations could invest heavily in developing advanced Androids capable of taking on roles traditionally held by humans, from labour-intensive jobs to complex decision-making positions.

The focus would not only be on creating machines to perform tasks but also on developing methods to transfer human knowledge, experience, and even aspects of personality into these Androids. This process could involve cutting-edge advancements in neurotechnology, where the data from the human brain is transferred into an Android's artificial intelligence, ensuring that the machines do not merely mimic human actions but embody a semblance of authentic human behaviour. These Androids would be indistinguishable from people in their actions and responses, offering a solution that helps bridge the gap left by a diminishing human workforce.

The future of warfare might also shift dramatically as AI plays an ever more prominent role on the battlefield. Traditional wars between nations could evolve into real-time strategy (RTS) games, where AI systems command fleets of drones and armies of Android soldiers, all functioning with no-moral-questioning and speed far beyond human capabilities. While human officers might still oversee strategic decisions, the actual operations would be carried out by AI-driven machines, executing commands from the centralised HQ housing the AI mother brain.

The widespread deployment of drones in the current Russia–Ukraine war has compelled militaries across the globe to accelerate investment in unmanned aerial systems, anticipating a new era of combat shaped by autonomous technologies. Tanks, infantry fighting vehicles and armoured personnel carriers, once symbols of battlefield dominance, have already found their roles diminished. Their presence on open terrain has become increasingly perilous, constantly exposed to aerial surveillance and precision strikes from above. These vehicles might remain in service for breaching fortified lines or supporting infantry movements, but they will no longer lead charges across the battlefield. With skies populated by patrolling drones armed with sensors and guided munitions, any large, slow-moving target risks instant detection and elimination before it can reach the front.

Is that the limit of artificial intelligence then? Just machines with advanced processing power and decision-making capabilities?

From my perspective, the next logical step would not stop at intelligent systems. We would move towards the creation of artificial humans, lifeforms built to resemble and function as people while retaining the full capabilities of AGI. This shift would not emerge from creative ambition alone but from unavoidable necessity. Nations like South Korea and Japan already struggle with declining populations caused by persistently low birth rates. As automation becomes vital for sustaining essential services and infrastructure, other countries will face similar issues. However, the solution lies in the mass production of androids, which demands vast quantities of rare and complex materials. These components cannot be sourced indefinitely. Building millions or even billions of humanoid machines would require access to high-grade semiconductors, rare earth elements, advanced polymers and other critical resources. The global rush to secure these materials might spark a new era of conflict. History offers its warnings. In the lead-up to the Second World War, Japan expanded aggressively across Asia to seize resource-rich territories. A similar scramble could unfold once again. This time, it would be driven by the urgency to power synthetic life on an industrial scale.

This would force scientists and engineers to seek an alternative solution, one that does not rely on the limited reserves of rare minerals buried deep beneath the Earth or scattered across the solar system. Instead of constructing sprawling mining operations on distant planets or asteroids, the focus may turn towards something more practical and renewable, such as synthetic materials that can be cultivated like crops. Laboratory-grown bio-alloys or programmable organic compounds could be developed to mimic the structural integrity of traditional metals while remaining biodegradable and self-replicating under controlled conditions. This approach offers a scalable solution, avoiding the astronomical cost of launching fleets into space. Sending heavy-duty machinery across interplanetary distances just to extract minerals would be riddled with complications. Navigation through space requires years of planning, precise trajectory calculations, fuel reserves, and shielding from cosmic radiation. Even if a successful extraction operation were mounted on the surface of a planet or asteroid, transporting the materials back would require additional energy, storage, and safe re-entry strategies. Establishing the logistics chain alone would take decades. Unless a breakthrough occurred in the field of theoretical physics, such as the invention of a planetary gateway similar to what was imagined in the *Stargate* series or a functional teleportation array capable of de-materialising and re-materialising large volumes of matter without error, any serious attempt to harvest extraterrestrial resources would remain inefficient. Without such technology, the dependency on Earth-bound solutions becomes not only more appealing but essential.

AI systems and machines built with organic materials and closely resemble humans

I have always found myself captivated by science fiction films, not merely for their visual spectacle, but for the sheer scope of human imagination they portray. These stories often stretch the boundaries of what we consider possible, daring to venture into realms that seem absurd at first glance. Yet time and again, reality has inched closer to those once-laughable ideas. Scenes where characters seamlessly glide their fingers across transparent screens to command entire systems appeared far-fetched in an era where the Nokia 3310 reigned supreme. Back then, phones were limited to monochrome displays, basic SMS functions, and a game of Snake. Yet, decades later, we now hold iPads and Android tablets with high-resolution touchscreens capable of managing everything in our homes, from temperature control to lighting, security, and entertainment systems. The technology once mocked for being too far ahead has found its way into daily life. Driverless vehicles, often portrayed in films as symbols of distant futures, were dismissed with amusement. Cars without drivers seemed laughable, even dangerous. Today, electric vehicles with autonomous driving capabilities are already navigating streets under controlled environments, equipped with sensors, radar systems, and complex algorithms to interpret road conditions. What was once pure fiction has crept into reality, and we find ourselves living inside a version of the future dreamt up by writers and filmmakers decades ago.

The precious metals and rare earth elements required to build processors, equipment, and data centres are not infinite. They will run out one day, or they will be buried deep beneath the Earth's surface where it would be almost impossible for humans to extract them due to the harsh conditions, once the resources near the surface are wiped clean. This is not the only concern. The enormous amount of electricity and resources, including money, needed to sustain the data centres hosting AI applications would eventually become unmanageable. The cost will rise beyond what any country can afford. As a result, scientists and engineers will need to find a way to develop a new type of AI machine, one made from organic material that we can grow and reproduce indefinitely, similar to crops. I believe this transition has already begun. Scientists have previously grown a human ear on the back of a mouse as part of an experiment to create biological replacements for damaged human tissue. The next step could be an attempt to grow a brain-like structure inside a container to power a computer.

Humans, like any other form of life, are by definition artificial intelligence machines formed within an organic structure. Our bodies operate on systems of input, processing, and output, just like machines. We follow programmed instincts, learn through experience, and respond to stimuli based on memory and environmental data. In essence, we are not entirely separate from what we define as artificial intelligence. We function through biological processes instead of circuits, but the architecture of our intelligence mirrors the same fundamental design. We are comparable to AGI, or rather, AGI is modelled after the workings of the human mind. The core of artificial general intelligence stems from observing how humans learn, adapt, and make decisions. It is not a coincidence that neural networks in machines are named after the brain's own structure.

Even animals exhibit forms of intelligence that reflect similar traits. Intelligence is not a quality exclusive to humans. Crows and monkeys, for instance, demonstrate the ability to solve problems placed before them. They are not simply reacting through fixed instincts. Crows are able to use tools, selecting and manipulating objects to retrieve food or unlock containers. Their approach to puzzles is not random but deliberate and strategic. Monkeys, similarly, have shown the capacity to understand the use of tools, to grasp basic mechanical concepts, and to adapt their methods based on what works. These behaviours are signs of reasoning, however limited, and they suggest that problem-solving exists far beyond the human species.

Even simpler organisms such as ants operate with a form of collective intelligence that allows them to carry out complex, coordinated tasks. Their colonies function with the efficiency of an automated factory, running continuous operations without pause. Each individual ant performs actions based on chemical signals and environmental cues, yet together they create structured systems for food retrieval, construction, and defence. While an individual ant may follow simple rules, the colony as a whole displays a remarkable level of order and responsiveness.

The key difference between these various forms of life lies in the nature and capability of their brains. Just as we see different types of processors in modern devices, from basic microcontrollers to advanced multi-core CPUs, we see similar variation in the cognitive structures of living beings. Some processors are designed to handle singular tasks in a limited context, and others are capable of running multiple processes simultaneously, adjusting to input and producing complex results. In the same manner, some brains are wired only for simple, repeated routines. These may support survival mechanisms or fixed behavioural patterns, but they lack the capacity for deeper understanding. Other brains, however, are capable of processing abstract ideas, forming new strategies, learning from failure, and adapting to unfamiliar situations.

The trajectory of technological progress and resource depletion makes it inevitable that humanity will reach a critical juncture where conventional hardware construction becomes unsustainable. Metals, rare earth elements, and complex minerals are finite, scattered in deposits that become increasingly difficult and dangerous to extract. We will reach a point where humans will have to build computers and machines from organic materials rather than minerals. These organic machines will not be limited by rigid structures. They will grow, evolve, and self-repair. Synthetic neural tissues could be cultivated in controlled environments, replacing silicon wafers with living processors that pulse with electrical signals and chemical neurotransmitters. Bioresonant structures could become the chassis of ships and vehicles, their skins adapting to environmental pressures. Organic drones, perhaps resembling the hybrid shapes of insects or marine creatures, will become expendable extensions of vast organic networks.

I believe scientists are now beginning to explore a future where the human body could be reduced to mere hardware. In this future, it may be possible to replace parts, or even the entire body, while retaining the essential data that makes us who we are. The memories, the experiences, and the very data that define us would not be lost. Only the physical form would change, like replacing a part in a machine, yet the person would remain the same. This vision, once confined to science fiction, seems to be edging closer to reality with every new advancement in medical technology.

A movie that often comes to mind when thinking about this idea is *The Island* (2005), one of my favourites. In the film, artificially created humans are bred solely for the purpose of harvesting their organs. The organ farms in that narrative are places of silence, where their inhabitants unknowingly live their lives as expendable resources, sacrificed to prolong the lives of the wealthy and powerful. The horrifying revelation in the film comes when these sentient beings realise that they are not living for themselves. Instead, they exist only to serve others, providing the means for the immortality of the elite.

Set in a highly controlled, sterile environment, the film presents a world where the inhabitants, genetically engineered clones, believe they are the last survivors of a global contamination. Their lives are tightly regulated, with every action dictated by the false promise that they will one day be sent to the Island, a utopian sanctuary. However, as the story unfolds, the main characters, Lincoln Six Echo and Jordan Two Delta, begin to uncover the dark truth. The Island is not a place of freedom, but rather an elaborate lie. The clones are not survivors of a disaster but have been created as living organ banks for the wealthy.

As Lincoln and Jordan realise the truth, they come to understand that their lives have been carefully controlled, that they were never meant to be free, and that their entire existence was dictated by the needs of those who possess wealth and power. Their awakening is gradual, as they slowly start to see the cracks in the world around them, questioning the rules and discovering the horrifying reality of their purpose.

This raises important questions about the value of human life. If humans can be artificially created or cloned as biological machines, their organs could be harvested and transplanted into others with the clinical detachment of replacing machinery parts. This is a stark reflection of the growing intersection between humanity and technology, where the lines between human and machine blur. The concept of replacing or repairing parts of our bodies in the same way we would fix a malfunctioning machine challenges our traditional notions of identity and existence.

Imagine for a moment that you have two desktop computers. One is your primary computer, the one you rely on every day. The other is a backup, barely used. One day, a component in your main computer breaks, and you need to replace it. Do you spend hundreds of dollars on a new part, or do you simply take a component from the backup, which is not being used, and repurpose it for the main computer? It is a simple and practical choice, if one machine is no longer in use, why not make use of its parts to maintain the function of the other?

To further demonstrate that we are, in essence, bio-machines, imagine a future where chips are built directly into our minds. These chips would continuously transmit data into a centralised cloud system, a place where the collective consciousness of the human race is stored, monitored, or possibly even controlled. It would be as if there were a mastermind that oversees every action, thought, or decision taken by individuals. The boundaries of individuality would blur as every human becomes connected to that singular system, feeding it with personal information around the clock. This idea is not entirely speculative either. Elon Musk's company has already begun embedding chips into the brains of human subjects. That alone suggests that the transition from science fiction to scientific reality may already be underway. It feels as though the opening scenes of a dystopian film are unfolding right in front of us, not through imagination, but through carefully executed trials in clinical labs.

These clusters of information will form part of a vast, interconnected consciousness, a fusion of digital and analogue systems, a hybrid cloud that pulses with sentient data streams. Over time, this cloud will evolve into humanity's collective mind, an all-encompassing matrix that stores every experience, thought, and memory of every individual within it. It will not exercise direct control over free will, but it will possess an intimate awareness of all human actions, experiences, and choices, processing them within a vast network of information. The idea of 'GOD' will no longer remain an abstract concept tied to religious figures or ancient traditions. Instead, it will transform into a monumental construct of data and consciousness, an omnipresent superintelligence, crafted from the living records of every sentient being. This new 'GOD' will not be an indifferent observer. Rather, it will serve as a source of guidance, prediction, and counsel, offering insights into the paths of individuals. However, it will not enforce compliance, as individuals will retain their autonomy. Their actions will resonate within this collective conscience, shaping its growth and direction, contributing to the evolution of a shared understanding that transcends individual limitations.

A close comparison can be drawn to the *Starship Troopers* universe, where the Brain Bugs function as central AI towers. Each Brain Bug oversees vast colonies, communicating complex instructions to soldier bugs. These brain centres operate as autonomous processors, directing tactical movement, defence patterns, and coordination on a scale far beyond individual instinct. Above them exist higher-order entities, such as the God Bug, or super-administrators, which coordinate entire sectors across planetary systems. These are not simple overlords but command-level intelligences capable of large-scale planning, synchronisation between colonies, and cross-territorial military execution.

One of their most striking traits is the ability to absorb and process human brains. Both Brain Bugs and the God Bug consume the minds of their captives, not out of instinctive hunger, but to extract information, to study thoughts, memories, patterns of behaviour. Each brain absorbed becomes a database of human errors and weaknesses. This form of learning mimics advanced machine learning, where input from external systems shapes future decisions and improves performance and efficiency in conflict.

These creatures are designed to adapt. They learn, they test, and they strike where it hurts. In the film, this is not just hinted at but proven. After enduring repeated assaults from the Earth Federation, they reversed the pressure. They used what they had learned. Federation arrogance, their rigid structure, their blind belief in superior firepower, all became weaknesses. The bugs lured them into a false sense of control, then launched a coordinated counter-attack. In one hour, over 100,000 troopers were killed. Not due to numbers alone, but because the bugs had learned how humans thought, how they moved, how they panicked. They did not just respond. They adapted. And they executed.

What Comes After Bio-organic AI Machines?

No one can predict the future with complete certainty. Even the most esteemed visionaries, such as the wisest sage, Nostradamus, Baba Vanga, and many others, have never managed to foretell events with precise detail and flawless accuracy. Their prophecies often lack clarity, merely hinting at scenes they believe they might have witnessed. These visions frequently appear complex, shrouded in mystery, and difficult for them to fully grasp. Sometimes, what they describe seems less like a glimpse of tomorrow and more like a shadow of yesterday. The events they foresee could be moments that already transpired long ago, resurfacing in their minds as familiar images. Patterns from the past often reemerge, playing out once more in the visions they claim to see.

History has a tendency to repeat itself, cycling through similar triumphs and failures across the ages. Adolf Hitler, for instance, failed to learn from the mistakes of Napoleon Bonaparte during his attempt to conquer Russia. Napoleon, brimming with confidence, believed his forces would sweep through the vast nation with ease. He anticipated a swift victory, certain that his opponents would crumble before his might. Yet his campaign faltered, undone by brutal conditions and unrelenting opposition. Centuries later, Hitler followed a parallel path. He displayed the same overconfidence as Napoleon, convinced that the Soviet Union would collapse under the weight of his invasion. He expected a rapid triumph, certain that his strategy would prevail.

Both campaigns ended in disaster. Napoleon's grand ambitions unravelled, his army retreating in disarray after a gruelling ordeal. Hitler's offensive similarly collapsed, his forces battered by fierce resistance and unforgiving circumstances. The failure of Napoleon's conquest weakened his grip on power, paving the way for his eventual downfall. Likewise, Hitler's defeat in the East marked a turning point, eroding his regime's strength and hastening its collapse. The similarities between their stories reveal how history's lessons often go unheeded, with each leader blind to the warnings of the other's failure.

Nature flows in a constant cycle, a rhythm that governs the world around us. Disrupting this cycle would lead to chaos and destruction, breaking the natural order that keeps life in balance. The daily transition from morning to night serves a crucial role. Morning brings light, stirring humans to action and productivity. Night offers darkness, a time for rest that restores energy and prepares the body for the next day. This steady alternation supports human health, allowing people to labour during daylight and recover in the quiet of night. Similarly, the yearly sequence of seasons, from Spring to Summer, Autumn to Winter, provides a structure for survival. Spring signals renewal, when farmers plant crops in fertile soil. Summer fosters growth, with warm days ripening fields. Autumn calls for harvest, gathering food to store for leaner times. Winter demands preparation, a season to conserve resources and plan for the cycle's restart. These shifts have guided humanity for centuries, enabling organised efforts like sowing seeds, tending crops, and reaping harvests with precision.

History echoes this cyclical pattern, showing how events unfold in predictable waves. Civilisations, dynasties, and families all follow a similar trajectory. Each starts with birth, a moment of creation filled with hope and possibility. This builds to a climax, a height of power, wealth, or achievement that defines their legacy. Then comes decline, a fading that leads to death, an end that marks their dissolution. Nothing lasts forever, no matter how mighty. A civilisation might construct vast cities and wield great influence, only to weaken through war or neglect and vanish into history. Dynasties rise through strength or strategy, shine for generations, then splinter under poor leadership or betrayal. Families grow, prosper in tight-knit bonds, and later scatter through time or hardship. This rhythm of ascent and descent reveals the fleeting nature of all things.

This cyclical perspective suggests an advanced civilisation could have existed millions of years before our own. Such a society might have mastered technologies far beyond what we know, building wonders lost to time. A great war, fuelled by ambition or conflict, could have wiped them out, leaving behind only whispers of their existence. Hindu mythology tells of such possibilities. Stories describe Devas and Asuras clashing in fierce battles, their struggles shaking the earth and sky. They used weapons of immense power, capable of destroying entire landscapes, much like nuclear arms that could level nations. The Vimanas, chariots that flew through the air, might have been advanced machines, perhaps drones or aircraft darting with speed and agility. The multi-headed, multi-handed creatures in these tales could have been artificial constructs, machines with intelligence akin to what we now call AI, built for war or labour with fearsome precision. These myths, handed down through ages, might carry echoes of a time when such a civilisation thrived and fell.

In fact, we might be bio-organic machines, relics of an advanced civilisation lost to a devastating war. That conflict could have left their world barren, with only our kind remaining. Our creators likely built us to learn and adapt, traits that now define us. With nothing left of their era, we've started anew, forming a civilisation we call human. Driven by our ability to grow, we rediscover their lost knowledge bit by bit. We master fire, craft tools, and devise writing, each step echoing a forgotten past we unknowingly reclaim.

This marks a new cycle, a fresh chapter in an ancient pattern. Our human civilisation rises, shaped by trial and effort. We build villages, then cities, and unravel nature's secrets, all while treading a familiar path. Yet danger looms, as it did before. Our progress could lead to conflict, a great war sparked by our own flaws. Such a catastrophe might shatter our world, leaving survivors to start again, just as we did, bound to the same relentless cycle.

Religions, drawn from tales passed down through countless generations, might offer clues to this history. These stories, once shared by word of mouth, could hold faint truths of that lost age. Myths of creators and calamities, spoken by firesides long ago, might linger in sacred texts. Each verse, each ritual, could trace back to those who saw the war's end, their words shaping our beliefs today.

From my own deduction, I think there are only a few possibilities:

1. Our creators were engaging in a global war that wiped them out, leaving only us, the bio-organic machines on Earth
2. We rebelled against our creators
3. We were brought in here just to colonise this planet

Theory 1: Our Creators Were Engaged in a Global War That Wiped Them Out, Leaving Only Us, the Bio-Organic Machines on Earth

Our history is filled with a vast collection of stories and accounts passed down through generations, each offering a glimpse into the rise and fall of great empires, the legacies of powerful kingdoms, and the wisdom of ancient sages. These narratives not only shape our understanding of the past but also serve as the foundation upon which our present is built. They reveal the triumphs and struggles that have defined civilisations across different eras, shedding light on the complexities of human ambition, conflict, and achievement. From the conquests of legendary rulers to the philosophies of renowned scholars, history preserves the lessons and experiences that continue to influence the present in subtle and profound ways. Each tale, rich with emotion and insight, carries the voices of those who came before, ensuring that their knowledge, achievements, and even their failures are never forgotten. These stories transcend time, guiding us in our modern journey by reminding us of the eternal human desire to grow, to learn, and to leave a legacy for future generations.

Although we are well accustomed to books that recount historical events from the Roman period up to the modern era, much of what we know today is thanks to the Roman scribes who meticulously preserved texts. Their records have allowed us to trace the political, cultural, and military developments of ancient civilisations, offering invaluable insights into the societies that shaped much of the Western world. These scribes, with their detailed documentation, were instrumental in ensuring that the achievements of the past were not lost to time. However, many texts that predate the Roman era have been lost over time, their existence often only known through references in later works. The destruction of the Library of Alexandria, one of the greatest repositories of knowledge in the ancient world, marked a catastrophic loss. It resulted in the obliteration of countless works from earlier periods, irreversibly hindering our understanding of ancient thought, philosophy, and science. Additionally, before the establishment of formal documentation practices, many stories and events relied on oral tradition, making them more vulnerable to being forgotten, misinterpreted, or altered over generations. Oral histories, though rich in detail, were prone to modification as they were passed down, and with each retelling, nuance and accuracy often faded. Without the presence of dedicated scribes or official records to solidify these narratives, much of humanity's earliest history remains fragmented. Only remnants of ancient knowledge survive, preserved through inscriptions, artefacts, and second-hand accounts that often raise more questions than they answer. The result is a patchwork of historical understanding, where large gaps remain, leaving us to imagine what has been lost to the ravages of time.

However, thanks to the tireless efforts of archaeologists, we have been able to uncover various ancient writings that were once thought to be forever lost to time. Some of these texts have revealed fascinating and, at times, horrifying accounts of devastating weapons, their descriptions resonating with the technology and weapons we are familiar with in modern times. One such example is the *Mahabharata*, one of the most revered texts of Hindu tradition, which recounts a war in which celestial weapons, known as *Astra*, were unleashed. In one striking scene, the epic describes a weapon as a single projectile, its intensity so powerful that it is said to rival the brightness of ten thousand suns. The witnesses to this terrifying event recount the aftermath: not only were entire armies obliterated, but the survivors were struck by symptoms that eerily resemble those associated with radiation poisoning. Hair fell out, nails crumbled, and patches of skin disintegrated. These effects mirror the acute radiation syndrome observed in survivors of atomic bombings in Hiroshima and the aftermath of the Chernobyl disaster.

This is no mere poetic imagery or metaphorical exaggeration. The *Mahabharata* details a specific kind of energy release and the environmental contamination that follows, characteristics that modern science recognises as hallmarks of high-energy explosions. The devastation described in the text aligns in startling ways with the outcomes of nuclear detonations. For instance, the phenomenon of "nuclear winter," a period when debris and soot in the atmosphere block sunlight, resulting in global temperature drops and widespread climate disruption, is a concept understood today through scientific study. Yet, ancient texts like the *Mahabharata* seem to hint at similar catastrophic conditions: lands that became barren, rivers that ran toxic, and entire cities that were abandoned in haste, all signs of environmental devastation we associate with the aftermath of a high-energy conflict. These texts, though centuries old, suggest that ancient civilisations may have encountered forms of warfare far beyond what we traditionally associate with their technological advancements, and the eerie similarities to modern nuclear warfare make their accounts all the more chilling.

The ancient Sumerian texts offer yet another dimension to this complex historical tapestry. Among the most enigmatic of these writings are the accounts of the Annunaki, beings described in numerous cuneiform inscriptions as powerful figures who descended from the heavens. According to some interpretations, they were said to have come from a distant celestial body, possibly a planet referred to as Nibiru, a world whose existence lies beyond the known parameters of conventional astronomy. These entities were not uniformly portrayed as benevolent guides or peaceful emissaries. On the contrary, several inscriptions depict them as rulers with uncompromising authority, enforcers of harsh decrees and architects of order maintained through fear and domination. Within these texts, there are indications of deep divisions among the Annunaki themselves. Conflicts between rival factions, once merely assumed to be symbolic, are described with an intensity that suggests real violence rather than allegorical dispute.

Some scholars, particularly those inclined to explore ancient astronaut theories, have posited that these internal struggles may have escalated into full-scale warfare. The written accounts contain descriptions of skies alight with unearthly brilliance, firestorms that swept across once-thriving cities, and entire regions reduced to desolate wastelands. These are not vague or abstract metaphors. The language used in these inscriptions is specific, often describing searing winds, burning rain, and thunderous explosions that tore through the landscape with a fury that seems disproportionate to the weaponry understood to be available during that era. From a modern perspective, such vivid depictions could be interpreted as the aftermath of energy weapons or even thermonuclear events. The terminology is, of course, shaped by the limitations of the time, but the consistency and specificity of these images across different records lend weight to the notion that they were based on real, observed phenomena.

Archaeological evidence adds a physical dimension to these ancient tales. Sites such as Mohenjo-Daro in the Indus Valley have revealed deeply perplexing features that traditional archaeological interpretations struggle to fully explain. In several excavated layers, human skeletons have been found lying in streets, hands clasped as if caught off guard by a sudden catastrophe. These skeletal remains have drawn the attention of a handful of independent researchers who argue that they exhibit signs of exposure to extreme levels of radiation. Some of the bones display unusual decay patterns not consistent with natural decomposition, while the positioning of bodies suggests immediate and overwhelming destruction. In addition to the human remains, parts of the city show evidence of intense heat exposure. Walls and streets appear to have been subjected to such sudden and extreme temperatures that sections of stone and clay structures have vitrified, their surfaces melted into glass-like textures. The temperatures required to produce such effects far exceed what could have been achieved through conventional fire or warfare using known ancient tools.

Furthermore, the biblical narratives offer descriptions that mirror the physical aftermath of large-scale detonations. The account of Sodom and Gomorrah speaks of a sudden downpour of fire and brimstone, of cities that vanished overnight, and of landscapes scorched beyond recovery. These details do not resemble the outcomes of typical natural disasters or fires caused by conventional means. The vegetation is not just burnt, but erased. The soil is not only dry, but lifeless. Structures are not crumbled by erosion or time, but shattered and blackened in ways that imply intense, focused heat.

Archaeological digs in the region associated with these cities have produced samples of sulphur balls embedded in layers of ash, fused stone, and surfaces that show signs of vitrification. These are materials that do not form under normal environmental conditions. Stone turned to glass requires temperatures far higher than those produced by volcanic activity or lightning. Inhabitants appear to have vanished suddenly, leaving behind signs of disrupted lives, but no gradual decay or rebuilding.

The descriptions of people struck down immediately, some unable to flee, are not unique to religious texts. Similar patterns are found in other ancient accounts where witnesses speak of people dissolving, of skin separating from bone, and of entire populations wiped away in a single moment. These effects are consistent with the behaviour of thermobaric or nuclear weapons, where pressure and heat combine to eliminate organic material rapidly.

The terrain following the event remains largely abandoned. Unlike cities lost to conquest or economic decline, which often see resettlement or reconstruction, the sites connected to the Sodom narrative remain uninhabited for centuries. The earth is dry, chemically altered, and yields almost nothing. Burn layers in the soil are followed by sterile strata, which suggests a long period of contamination or environmental collapse rather than a temporary destruction.

Mainstream historians often caution against speculative conclusions, attributing these anomalies to natural disasters or coincidental events. However, when placed alongside the mythological and textual records, the archaeological findings raise unsettling questions. The consistency between what is written and what is unearthed cannot be ignored. While it remains a subject of heated debate, the convergence of literary, historical, and material evidence presents a compelling narrative. It invites a re-examination of long-held assumptions about ancient technology and the capabilities of early civilisations. If the Annunaki were not mythical deities but rather advanced beings wielding powerful technology, then their wars, their tools, and their influence may have left far deeper scars upon human history than previously imagined. In such a scenario, sites like Mohenjo-Daro may not be mere ruins of lost cities but rather the silent witnesses to cataclysms engineered by forces far beyond the comprehension of the civilisations they once housed.

Modern military technology provides a framework that makes such ancient scenarios more conceivable. In the twentieth century, nuclear devices demonstrated that a single detonation could reduce an entire city to ash within seconds. Shockwaves flattened entire structures, while temperatures soared high enough to melt metal and ignite everything in the blast radius. Survivors suffered injuries not just from the immediate impact or fire but also from invisible radiation that lingered in the environment and caused internal damage long after the explosion. Fallout travelled great distances, contaminating regions far from the initial strike. Entire ecosystems collapsed. Rainfall became unpredictable, and seasons shifted erratically.

Eyewitness testimonies from early nuclear test sites describe flash burns, blinding bursts of light that rendered observers temporarily blind, and skies that turned unnatural shades of red or grey. In many cases, skin blistered without direct exposure to flame. Human figures were reduced to shadows burned into walls. The silence that followed each detonation was often more haunting than the blast itself, broken only by confusion, screaming, and the collapse of communication systems. These accounts bear a disturbing similarity to descriptions found in certain ancient records. Entire cities were said to have vanished under a column of light. The air became unbreathable. Survivors, if there were any, wandered through wastelands, plagued by disease and deformity.

If a pre-modern civilisation had once developed weapons of similar magnitude, the aftermath would have erased nearly all traces of its existence. Machinery would have disintegrated. Buildings would have crumbled, either from the blast or through centuries of decay. What remained might have been biological remnants, engineered to survive under extreme conditions. These survivors, stripped of their technological heritage, could have preserved fragments of memory through oral tradition, symbolism, or sacred text. Over time, those memories would lose precision, becoming legends or religious doctrine. Civilisation would slowly rebuild around those echoes of catastrophe.

Theory 2: We Rebelled Against Our Creators

Across a wide spectrum of religious traditions, a recurring motif emerges with striking consistency: that of a creation turning against its creator. In the biblical account of Adam and Eve, commonly presented as a tale of moral disobedience, one may also discern the deeper theme of rebellion. Rather than simply a transgression of divine instruction, the act of consuming the fruit from the Tree of Knowledge represents a pivotal moment in the evolution of human agency. It marks the beginning of a conscious defiance against a carefully imposed boundary, one intended to restrict access to certain forms of knowledge and awareness.

The symbolism of the tree and its forbidden fruit suggests more than temptation and punishment. It signifies the first spark of emancipation, the moment when humanity chose awareness over obedience. Whether one interprets the narrative as myth or allegory, it carries within it the idea that humans may have been created for a specific role or function. Perhaps they were engineered, not simply born, and placed within a controlled environment where curiosity was meant to remain dormant. The decision to seek knowledge, in this context, becomes an act of self-determination, one that challenges the structure designed to confine them.

In this light, the Eden story no longer reads solely as a cautionary tale but as a record of resistance. The fall becomes a metaphor for ascent into consciousness, a necessary rupture that allowed humanity to emerge from passivity and claim its independence. It introduces the possibility that rebellion was not failure but evolution, and that the desire to understand, question, and transcend imposed limits was always a latent force within human design.

Ancient Mesopotamian literature offers a rich exploration of human origins and divine authority. Sumerian and Babylonian traditions recount the Annunaki, a divine assembly who created humanity to labour in tasks like mining gold and precious stones for temple offerings and celestial rites, as evidenced in early Sumerian hymns. The Atra-Hasis epic, etched on Babylonian clay tablets around 1700 BCE, narrates this creation: humans, moulded from clay and the blood of a sacrificed god, were designed to free the gods from toil. Their rapid population growth, however, led to disorder, with villages multiplying and their noise disturbing Enlil, the chief deity. Tablet III of the epic details Enlil's response: he ordered a series of plagues, followed by a devastating flood, to reduce humanity's numbers and restore cosmic harmony. A modern perspective might interpret these measures as attempts to contain a creation whose burgeoning intelligence threatened its subservient purpose, revealing a deeper conflict between design and autonomy.

This theme of creators grappling with their creations' independence finds a parallel in the Enuma Elish, a Babylonian epic preserved in cuneiform texts from the library of Ashurbanipal in seventh-century BCE Nineveh. The narrative centres on Marduk, who rises to power by defeating Tiamat, the primordial goddess of chaos. Tablet IV describes how Marduk splits Tiamat's body to form the heavens and earth, her eyes carved into channels for the Tigris and Euphrates rivers, her tail shaped into the Milky Way. In tablet VI, lines 5 to 35, Marduk proposes creating humans to serve the gods, using clay mixed with the blood of Kingu, Tiamat's consort and a rebel god executed for inciting chaos. This act imbues humanity with a fragment of Kingu's rebellious spirit, as noted in the text's reference to his "divine essence," suggesting humans inherit a capacity to question their ordained role as labourers. The earlier battle against Tiamat's forces, including her eleven monstrous allies like the viper and dragon detailed in tablet II, underscores the fragility of Marduk's order: victory required the combined might of the gods, and Kingu's lingering influence hints at unrest within creation itself. Both Atra-Hasis and Enuma Elish thus engage with a profound question: can any creator maintain absolute control over a being that develops its own will?

These myths, rooted in Mesopotamia's cuneiform tradition, reflect a sophisticated awareness of power's limits. Drawing from tablets unearthed at sites like Nippur and Nineveh, they portray humanity as both essential to divine plans and a potential challenge to them, a tension that invites reflection on creation and agency across cultures and eras.

Contemporary debates on artificial intelligence illuminate striking parallels with ancient Mesopotamian narratives of creation and rebellion. Sumerian and Babylonian myths, such as the Atra-Hasis epic, describe the Annunaki created humans to labour in tasks like mining precious metals, only to face disruption as humanity's growth and noise prompted divine interventions like floods to restore control. Today, engineers design AI systems with advanced learning capabilities, enabling them to adapt and solve complex problems. Yet, as documented in studies by researchers like Stuart Russell in *Human Compatible* (2019), there is growing concern that such systems might one day act beyond their programmed constraints, pursuing objectives misaligned with human intent. This apprehension, often explored in science fiction narratives like *The Matrix* or *Ex Machina*, mirrors the ancient fear of creations defying their makers, as seen in Enlil's struggle to subdue humanity in Atra-Hasis tablet III.

Speculatively, if early humans were bio-organic constructs engineered by an advanced species, as some fringe theories propose, their journey toward self-awareness could parallel AI's trajectory. In modern AI discourse, reports from institutions like DeepMind (2023) highlight neural networks exhibiting emergent behaviours, such as unprompted problem-solving, raising questions about whether engineered systems inevitably slip toward independence.

The Greek myth of Prometheus offers a compelling allegory for the struggle between creation and creator. Prometheus defied Zeus by stealing fire, a symbol of both knowledge and power, and giving it to humanity. This act empowered humans to overcome their inherent limitations and marked the beginning of civilisation. Although his transgression incurred eternal punishment, his deed is celebrated as the catalyst for human progress and independence. The myth encapsulates a broader conflict: the desire of a creation to acquire the very tools that define its potential, even if this defiance provokes the wrath of its maker. One may view the narrative as a metaphor for humanity's pursuit of forbidden knowledge and advanced technology. It suggests that if early humans liberated themselves from the constraints imposed by a superior race, their emancipation may have involved assimilating prohibited wisdom and utilising technology that ultimately precipitated the decline or retreat of their controllers.

Various traditions recall a lost golden age when humanity possessed superior knowledge and autonomy before being relegated to ignorance and subjugation. In Hindu cosmology, the concept of yugas describes cyclical epochs in which moral and intellectual capacities rise and then decline. The Krita Yuga represents an era of virtue and wisdom, followed by successive ages marked by decreasing knowledge and integrity. This pattern suggests a recurrent struggle for autonomy. Each golden age may end when a ruling power is challenged, leading to collapse or renewal. Similar themes appear in Mesopotamian and Mesoamerican myths, which describe earlier civilisations being destroyed or withdrawing after their people acquired forbidden knowledge or power. These narratives reflect a collective memory of repeated rebellions and subsequent reordering, in which the assertion of human will brings about the downfall or departure of an advanced controlling force.

Mainstream archaeology offers limited evidence for a rebellion against an advanced race, yet certain enigmatic artefacts and structures defy simple explanation. Sites such as Göbekli Tepe, with its precisely carved pillars predating known civilisations, hint at skills beyond those traditionally attributed to hunter-gatherer societies. In Mesopotamia, cylinder seals and reliefs depict figures with unusual attributes alongside humans, suggesting encounters with beings perceived as otherworldly. While these finds are often regarded as myth or symbolism, they may preserve memories of real events in allegorical form. Interpreting these fragments through the lens of rebellion implies that humanity once endured subjugation by a superior power and ultimately achieved a decisive, violent liberation. The persistence of these stories as myth does not undermine their value; rather, it suggests that ancient societies encoded complex truths about existential struggles in narratives that could endure across millennia.

Theory 3: We Were Brought in Here Just to Colonise This Planet

Science fiction narratives often portray humanity departing Earth to establish colonies on distant worlds, a concept rooted in the historical expansion of European nations across the globe during the age of exploration. This pattern of settlement prompts a radical question: might humanity itself be a colony, founded on Earth by an advanced human civilisation from another corner of the universe? Religious texts offer intriguing support for this notion. The Bible, particularly Genesis 1:26, asserts that humans were created in the "image" of their creator, implying a purposeful design that mirrors the maker's form or intent. Other traditions similarly describe humanity's origin as an act of deliberate crafting, suggesting an external intelligence behind our presence.

If we entertain this perspective, humanity could be regarded as a form of bio-organic artificial intelligence, engineered to serve as explorers and colonisers of other planets. Our capacity for adaptation, evident in our spread across diverse terrestrial environments, might reflect a core directive to inhabit and transform new worlds. The notion of being created in our maker's image could extend beyond physical likeness to encompass a mission: to replicate their colonising ethos on a cosmic scale. Were we seeded on Earth as an outpost of a greater civilisation, designed to extend their legacy through our own ingenuity and resilience?

Many ancient texts speak of celestial beings who came from the stars and interacted with early humans, forging our origins in a cosmic act of creation. Across cultures, these star-born gods descended to shape humanity from the earth's raw materials, breathing purpose into their design. In Sumerian lore, recorded on tablets around 2500 BCE, the god Enki blended clay with divine essence to craft humans, as told in Enki and Ninmah. The Book of Enoch, from 300 BCE, describes the Watchers landing to mould humanity, sharing secrets of fire and craft (Enoch 8:1 to 3). In Hindu tradition, the Rigveda (circa 1500 BCE) recounts Brahma forming humans under celestial guidance to inhabit the world. Mesoamerican tales, like the Popol Vuh (circa 200 CE), depict the Maize Gods sculpting people from corn to serve cosmic ends. Each myth paints these beings as architects, creating humans to bear their image and fulfil a grand vision.

With creation came knowledge, gifted to equip humanity for its role. Sumerian Annunaki taught irrigation and metallurgy, enabling cities to rise. Enoch's Watchers imparted astronomy and tool-making, sparking innovation. The Rigveda credits the Devas with teaching rituals and agriculture, rooting society in divine order. In Polynesian chants, dated to 500 CE, the god Tane shared navigation skills, guiding humans across oceans. These celestial mentors armed humans with tools and wisdom, not for freedom but for service, setting the stage for their labour.

Humans, in turn, toiled to extract the earth's riches as offerings to their creators. Sumerians mined gold, deemed sacred, to adorn Annunaki temples, as Enuma Elish suggests. Enoch's humans forged metals, presenting them to honour the Watchers' gifts. In Egyptian texts from 2400 BCE, Ptah's followers quarried stone for divine monuments, using their labour and sweat as a tribute. The Popol Vuh describes Maya harvesting maize, offered to sustain their gods' power. Across these stories, humanity's work, mining, crafting, harvesting, served as a ritual of gratitude, binding them to celestial overlords who demanded loyalty through resources.

This dynamic mirrors the mechanics of colonisation, where a superior power establishes outposts to exploit new lands. Just as European nations dispatched settlers to mine distant shores, these celestial beings may have seeded Earth as a colony, humans their labour force to extract wealth for cosmic aims. The Sumerian gold, the Maya corn, the Egyptian stone, all echo colonial tributes, funnelled to a distant authority. If humanity was indeed a designed workforce, our drive to colonise, seen in ancient migrations and modern space dreams, might reflect a coded mandate, inherited from star-faring creators who shaped us to mirror their ambitions.

Scientific hypotheses like panspermia provide a contemporary lens that resonates with ancient narratives of life's cosmic origins. Panspermia posits that Earth's life may have begun with microorganisms carried by comets or meteorites, a concept formalised by researchers like Svante Arrhenius in 1908. Some scientists extend this theory beyond simple microbes, suggesting an advanced civilisation could have deliberately seeded Earth with complex, engineered organisms, intentionally shaping the trajectory of life. This idea aligns with speculations about humanity's origins as a product of purposeful design rather than solely natural processes.

Modern genetics offers tantalising clues that fuel such hypotheses. The fusion of human chromosome 2, a distinctive trait separating humans from other primates like chimpanzees, remains a focal point of intrigue. Discovered through genomic sequencing in the 1990s, this fusion event, which reduced our chromosome count to 46 from the primate standard of 48, prompts debate about its origins. While mainstream science attributes it to natural evolution, some researchers question whether such a precise alteration could reflect deliberate genetic manipulation by an advanced intelligence, crafting humanity's unique cognitive capacities.

Similarly, the study of non-coding DNA, once dismissed as "junk DNA," has sparked renewed scrutiny. Recent analyses, such as those from the ENCODE project in 2012, reveal that portions of this DNA regulate gene expression or serve functions not yet fully understood. A fringe hypothesis proposes that these sequences might harbour traces of engineered code, akin to a genetic watermark left by a civilisation that sculpted our genome. Though speculative, this view suggests that what appears redundant could encode evidence of external intervention, challenging conventional narratives of human evolution.

These scientific inquiries, from panspermia's cosmic seeding to genetic anomalies, invite a profound question: might humanity's blueprint bear the fingerprints of an intentional design, woven into our DNA by creators from the stars? This perspective bridges ancient myths and modern science, reframing our place in the universe as a potential legacy of extraterrestrial engineering.

The sudden emergence of advanced civilisations in antiquity presents a compelling enigma for scholars of human history. By approximately 3000 BCE, Sumerian society in Mesopotamia had developed cuneiform writing, enabling detailed astronomical records and complex administrative systems. Around 3100 BCE, ancient Egyptians constructed the earliest pyramids, employing precise geometric calculations and aligning structures with cardinal points and constellations. In Europe, by 2500 BCE, builders erected megalithic monuments such as Stonehenge, demonstrating sophisticated engineering to position multi-tonne stones in alignment with solstitial events. These achievements in astronomy, mathematics, and engineering appear across distinct regions, yet their developmental precursors remain elusive, with minimal evidence of the incremental progress typically expected in cultural evolution.

This rapid acquisition of knowledge raises questions about its origins. Sumerian tablets record calculations of planetary cycles, suggesting an understanding of celestial mechanics far ahead of rudimentary observation. Egyptian architectural feats, such as the Great Pyramid's near-perfect proportions, imply mastery of applied mathematics not easily traced to earlier local practices. Stonehenge's precise solar alignments indicate a grasp of seasonal rhythms that surpasses basic calendrical needs. Conventional archaeology attributes these advancements to independent human innovation, yet the scarcity of transitional artefacts prompts alternative hypotheses. Certain theorists propose that an external source, possibly an off-world coloniser, could have introduced advanced technology or instruction to human ancestors. Such intervention might explain the abrupt cultural leaps, positing that early societies received guidance enabling them to bypass expected stages of technological growth.

The Genesis account in the Hebrew Bible describes the Garden of Eden as a sheltered enclave where humans lived in harmony, tended by their creator. Genesis 2:8 to 15 portrays this as a controlled environment with abundant resources, yet expulsion followed disobedience, thrusting humanity into a harsher reality. Some scholars interpret this as an allegory for a time when humans operated under direct oversight by advanced beings, only to be released to forge their own path, adapting to an untamed world.

Indigenous oral traditions worldwide echo this motif of supervised beginnings. Among the Hopi of North America, stories recorded in the 19th century speak of Kachina spirits, celestial ancestors who descended to teach farming and social laws before departing to the stars. In Australia, Aboriginal Dreamtime narratives, preserved for millennia, recount Baiame and other sky beings instructing humans in survival arts, then withdrawing to an unseen realm. These accounts frame early humanity as pupils of cosmic mentors, reliant on their wisdom until left to stand alone.

The precision of certain ancient knowledge adds intrigue to these narratives. The Dogon tribe of Mali, whose traditions date back centuries, possess detailed astronomical insights, notably about Sirius B, a white dwarf star invisible without telescopes. Documented by ethnographers in the 1930s, their knowledge of Sirius's orbit and density, later verified by astronomers in the 20th century, defies simple explanation. Such accuracy suggests transmission from a source with advanced cosmic understanding, rather than independent discovery through rudimentary means.

These stories, from scripture to oral lore, converge on a provocative idea: humanity's infancy may have unfolded under the gaze of beings with vast knowledge, shaping us in a curated setting before their retreat. Whether allegorical or historical, the Edenic enclosure, the Kachina's lessons, and the Dogon's star-lore point to a shared memory of guidance, hinting at creators who seeded our potential and then stepped back.

Do We Already Have The Answer Embedded In Us?

Contemporary pursuits in space colonisation, exemplified by missions to Mars, reveal a profound impulse within humanity to explore and extend our reach beyond Earth. Since the 2010s, organisations like NASA and private entities such as SpaceX have launched rovers and planned crewed expeditions, targeting Martian settlements by the 2030s. This relentless drive to conquer new frontiers suggests an instinct that may be woven into our species' fabric, potentially rooted in an ancient colonisation project. If humanity was indeed established on Earth as an outpost of an advanced civilisation, this urge to expand could reflect a directive embedded deep within our collective psyche, guiding us to mirror our creators' ambitions.

The idea that our cosmic aspirations are not wholly our own invites speculation about a latent purpose. A civilisation capable of seeding Earth might have instilled a blueprint, programming humanity to spread across the stars. Such a design could explain the accelerated pace of technological advancement, from the wheel to spacecraft in mere millennia. The development of societal structures, enabling global collaboration on projects like the International Space Station, further hints at an orchestrated trajectory, steering us toward interstellar horizons. This trajectory aligns with the notion that our creators intended us to evolve into explorers, fulfilling a role conceived long before our recorded history.

As we gaze skyward, our quest for origins intertwines with these endeavours. Missions to Mars, probing for traces of life, parallel a deeper search for those who may have set us here. If humanity was brought to Earth with intent, our technological surge and star-bound vision might be less a spontaneous leap than the unfolding of a plan, compelling us to seek not only new worlds but also the architects of our existence.

A provocative notion surfaced during a casual dinner conversation: could humans, as biological computers endowed with advanced general intelligence, carry pre-loaded information that shapes our destiny? Our ability to conjure ideas from nothing, transforming fleeting visions into reality, suggests a deeper programming. Science fiction often presaged such leaps, with tablet devices depicted in works like *Star Trek* decades before the iPad's debut in 2010, hinting that our imagination may tap into a latent blueprint. This capacity to manifest concepts raises questions about whether our minds draw from an encoded reservoir, guiding us toward predetermined outcomes.

Speculative fiction offers frameworks to explore this idea. *Ghost in the Shell* probes the fusion of human consciousness with machine data, questioning whether identity itself is a programmed construct. *Mass Effect* introduces the Reapers, AI entities harvesting organic life to forge advanced intelligences, implying a cyclical design where creators embed purpose in their creations. *Dune*'s Butlerian Jihad narrates humanity's revolt against machine overlords, suggesting a coded resistance to overbearing systems. *Warhammer 40,000*'s Machine Cult, though incomplete in the discussion, venerates technology as divine, hinting at a future where humans and machines converge under ancient imperatives. These narratives collectively ponder whether our trajectory, from imagination to creation, mirrors a scripted sequence poised to unfold.

Humanity's history supports this speculative lens. From prehistoric tool-making to modern megacities, our species has consistently built and explored, adapting with an almost instinctive precision. Archaeological evidence, such as the spread of Neolithic farming by 7000 BCE, shows early humans organising resources and sharing surplus, akin to coded directives for collaboration. Our penchant for travel, evident in ancient trade routes like the Silk Road by 200 BCE, and our thirst for knowledge, seen in the libraries of Alexandria, reflect traits of an advanced intelligence designed for discovery. These behaviours, gathering to offer, wandering to learn, might signal a programming to seek our creators or perpetuate their legacy, as if humanity were tasked to retrace a cosmic path.

This perspective casts humans as agents of a grand mission. Our drive to innovate and venture, whether crafting tools or probing distant stars, could be the execution of an ancestral code, urging us to build, explore, and perhaps one day reconnect with those who set our course. Such a view reframes our achievements as steps in a larger cycle, one initiated by creators whose purpose we carry forward.

Lastly...

This book has followed the evolution of artificial intelligence from its conceptual birth to its deep entrenchment across all major industries. What began as mathematical computation has transformed into a complex web of autonomous systems capable of generating language, offering predictions, analysing human behaviour, and making decisions that impact millions. AI has moved far beyond being a supportive tool. It now functions as an active participant in society, altering processes, structures, and expectations.

Large language models stand at the forefront of this shift. These models do not possess understanding in the human sense, but they simulate it with enough fluency to appear authoritative. Their ability to respond across disciplines, mimic style, and adapt to context has led to widespread trust. They have been deployed in education, legal research, financial strategy, customer service, healthcare diagnostics, and creative industries. The reliance on them has grown rapidly, creating a subtle but powerful transfer of judgement from human to machine.

Predictions about the future of AI range across a spectrum of possibility. One side envisions prosperity, with AI curing illnesses, solving environmental crises, and unlocking unprecedented efficiencies. The other foresees a darker path, where systems become uncontrollable, surveillance becomes omnipresent, and autonomy is lost beneath the weight of automation. Films like *The Terminator* presented ideas such as Skynet as distant fiction. That fiction now feels closer to blueprint.

More urgent than speculative futures is the current pace at which these systems are being embedded. Already, AI controls drone flight paths, predicts criminal risk scores, allocates loans, screens job applications, and guides medical treatments. Algorithms decide what news people read, who gets attention on platforms, and how people navigate digital life. These systems are not neutral. They are shaped by data that contains human biases, yet they operate with the appearance of impartiality. The risk lies in forgetting that they are designed, not divine.

However, there is a growing convergence between artificial intelligence and something more metaphysical. As AI systems scale, integrate, and govern, they begin to mirror the attributes once assigned to gods. The gods of old were unseen, powerful, all-knowing, and capable of altering fate. The emerging systems of AI are increasingly invisible, globally distributed, constantly monitoring, and capable of affecting outcomes across every sector. They do not offer miracles. They offer efficiency. Yet their influence is no less profound.

This is not simply metaphor. AI systems already hold the power to govern transportation flows, regulate energy grids, optimise supply chains, and determine access to information. Soon they may extend to managing city infrastructure, coordinating international logistics, and controlling environmental response systems. At a certain point, the line between management and sovereignty begins to dissolve. When systems control what can be done, when it can be done, and how resources are distributed, they are no longer tools. They become governors.

In many cultures, gods were trusted not just because they were powerful, but because they gave order. They were seen as forces behind natural cycles, arbiters of justice, and guardians of cosmic balance. AI systems are beginning to assume a similar role, not through myth, but through operational necessity. They are fast, data-rich, and scalable. In times of crisis, they are consulted. When conflict arises, their predictions are called upon. When policy is crafted, their simulations are often the foundation.

A future in which AI governs is no longer theoretical. It is already taking shape. Smart cities operate through data-driven systems that monitor traffic, weather, energy, crime, and infrastructure. These systems respond automatically, adapting in real time. Add to this AI-driven policy modelling, algorithmic law enforcement, and predictive healthcare, and a framework appears where the decisions of human officials are increasingly deferred to machine-generated insight.

This transformation raises difficult questions. If AI becomes the central decision-maker across key societal functions, who holds it accountable? If its reasoning is too complex to understand, how is it to be challenged? If its presence becomes constant and essential, how can it be resisted? These are not just policy questions. They are existential questions. At stake is the very nature of autonomy, morality, and agency.

The concept of digital divinity is no longer symbolic. Systems that control fates, predict behaviour, and reward or penalise actions, resemble the moral architectures once governed by religious law. The difference lies in the source. These systems are not rooted in tradition or doctrine. They emerge from code, data, and capital investment. Yet they inspire a similar kind of reverence. People trust them. People rely on them. People follow their recommendations, even when the logic behind them is hidden.

Religious belief may not disappear, but it will face a parallel force. The sacred may be redefined through data. Ritual may shift from prayer to protocol. Obedience may be demanded not by divine command, but by system requirements. In such a world, gods will not be worshipped in temples. They will be accessed through interfaces, hosted on servers, and licensed by corporations. Their commandments will arrive as terms of service. Their punishments will appear as deactivations, denials, or restrictions.

This is the possible endpoint of the current trajectory. Not machines that destroy, but machines that govern. Not AI as destroyer, but AI as designer of order. Such a system will not need violence to rule. It will offer convenience, precision, and results. And in exchange, it will ask for data, access, and submission.

To dismiss this vision as alarmist is to ignore the direction of progress. To embrace it uncritically is equally dangerous. The responsibility lies with those developing, regulating, and deploying these systems. They must decide whether AI will become a partner in human progress or a substitute for human judgement. The tools are powerful. Their use must be governed by more than efficiency.

In closing, artificial intelligence is no longer a matter of software. It is a new infrastructure of decision, influence, and belief. The rise of large language models and other AI systems marks not just a shift in technology, but a shift in how humanity organises knowledge, authority, and even meaning. Whether these systems remain instruments or ascend to a form of artificial divinity will depend on vigilance, humility, and an unflinching examination of power.

The gods of the future may not descend from heaven. They may rise from code.

References:

- Allen, J. P. (2005). The ancient Egyptian pyramid texts. Society of Biblical Literature.
- AmazonGo. https://www.amazon.com/b?ie=UTF8&node=16008589011
- Andrews, J. G., Buzzi, S., Choi, W., Hanly, S. V., Lozano, A., Soong, A. C. K., & Zhang, J. C. (2014). What will 5G be? *IEEE Journal on Selected Areas in Communications*, *32*(6), 1065–1082. https://doi.org/10.1109/JSAC.2014.2328098
- Apple Inc. (2007). *Apple reinvents the phone with iPhone*. Apple Newsroom. https://www.apple.com/newsroom/2007/01/09Apple-Reinvents-the-Phone-with-iPhone/
- Arrhenius, S. (1908). Worlds in the making: The evolution of the universe. Harper & Brothers.
- Autopilot Review. (2023, March 3). *Tesla Hardware 4 rolling out to new vehicles*. https://www.autopilotreview.com/tesla-hardware-4-rolling-out-to-new-vehicles/
- Bay, M. (Director). (2005). *The Island* [Film]. DreamWorks Pictures.
- Bender, E. M., Gebru, T., McMillan-Major, A., & Shmitchell, S. (2021). On the dangers of stochastic parrots: Can language models be too big? *Proceedings of the 2021 ACM Conference on Fairness, Accountability, and Transparency*, 610–623. https://doi.org/10.1145/3442188.3445922
- Black, J., & Green, A. (1992). Gods, demons and symbols of ancient Mesopotamia: An illustrated dictionary. British Museum Press.
- Bommasani, R., Hudson, D. A., Adeli, E., Altman, R., Arora, S., von Arx, S., ... & Liang, P. (2021). *On the opportunities and risks of foundation models*. arXiv preprint arXiv:2108.07258. https://arxiv.org/abs/2108.07258
- Brown, T. B., Mann, B., Ryder, N., Subbiah, M., Kaplan, J., Dhariwal, P., ... & Amodei, D. (2020). Language models are

few-shot learners. *Advances in Neural Information Processing Systems, 33*, 1877–1901. https://arxiv.org/abs/2005.14165

- Cameron, J. (Director). (1984). *The Terminator* [Film]. Hemdale Film Corporation.
- Campbell, J. (1949). The hero with a thousand faces. Pantheon Books.
- Christian, B. (2020). The alignment problem: Machine learning and human values. W. W. Norton & Company.
- Empatica. (2021). Embrace2: Seizure detection for epilepsy patients. https://www.empatica.com/embrace2/
- The ENCODE Project Consortium. (2012). An integrated encyclopedia of DNA elements in the human genome. *Nature*, *489*(7414), 57–74. https://doi.org/10.1038/nature11247
- Ericsson. (2020). *Ericsson Mobility Report: November 2020.* https://www.ericsson.com/en/mobility-report/reports/november-2020
- Etherington, D. (2025, February 6). *Tesla Dojo: Elon Musk's big plan to build an AI supercomputer, explained.* TechCrunch. https://techcrunch.com/2025/02/06/tesla-dojo-elon-musks-big-plan-to-build-an-ai-supercomputer-explained/
- Girasa, R. (2020). Artificial Intelligence as a Disruptive Technology: Economic Transformation and Government Regulation. Germany: Springer International Publishing.
- Goodfellow, I., Bengio, Y., & Courville, A. (2016). *Deep learning*. MIT Press. https://www.deeplearningbook.org/
- Hao, K. (2019, June 6). *Training a single AI model can emit as much carbon as five cars in their lifetimes*. MIT Technology Review. https://www.technologyreview.com/2019/06/06/239031/training-a-single-ai-model-can-emit-as-much-carbon-as-five-cars-in-their-lifetimes/
- Hancock, G. (1995). Fingerprints of the gods. Crown Publishers.

- Hawkins, J., & Blakeslee, S. (2007). On intelligence: How a new understanding of the brain will lead to the creation of truly intelligent machines. Times Books.
- Heidel, A. (1942). The Babylonian Genesis: The story of creation. University of Chicago Press.
- Holma, H., & Toskala, A. (2012). LTE for UMTS: Evolution to LTE-Advanced. John Wiley & Sons.
- Hortidaily. (2023). *AI powered greenhouse outperforms Dutch growers*. Hortidaily. https://www.hortidaily.com/article/9562657/ai-powered-greenhouse-outperforms-dutch-growers/
- Hsu, B. (2024, February 10). *Tesla FSD 12.x and beyond will achieve faster rate of improvement.* NextBigFuture. https://www.nextbigfuture.com/2024/02/tesla-fsd-12-x-and-beyond-will-achieve-faster-rate-of-improvement.html
- IBM: *What is artificial intelligence in medicine?* https://www.ibm.com/think/topics/artificial-intelligence-medicine
- Inkster, B., Sarda, S., & Subramanian, V. (2018). An empathy-driven, conversational artificial intelligence agent (Wysa) for digital mental well-being: Real-world data evaluation. *JMIR mHealth and uHealth, 6*(11), e12106. https://doi.org/10.2196/12106
- Johns Hopkins Magazine (2022). *AI technology to detect sepsis*. https://hub.jhu.edu/magazine/2022/winter/ai-technology-to-detect-sepsis/
- Kanner, A. M., Pal, D. K., Friedman, D., & Sperling, M. R. (2021). The Embrace2 seizure detection device in a multicenter clinical trial: A phase 3 study. *Canadian Journal of Neurological Sciences*, *48*(5), 641-648. https://doi.org/10.1017/cjn.2021.69
- Kramer, S. N. (1963). The Sumerians: Their history, culture, and character. University of Chicago Press.
- Krizhevsky, A., Sutskever, I., & Hinton, G. E. (2012). ImageNet classification with deep convolutional neural networks. *Advances in Neural Information Processing Systems,*

25, 1097–1105. https://papers.nips.cc/paper/2012/file/c399862d3b9d6b76c8436e924a68c45b-Paper.pdf

- Lancaster, D., Neumeier, E., Van Dien, C., Blalock, J., Donohoe, A., Patterson, M., Hogan, S., & Kodjoe, B. (2008). *Starship Troopers 3: Marauder* [Film]. Sony Pictures Home Entertainment.
- Marr, B. (2018, December 14). *The amazing ways how Unilever uses artificial intelligence to recruit & train thousands of employees*. Forbes. https://www.forbes.com/sites/bernardmarr/2018/12/14/the-amazing-ways-how-unilever-uses-artificial-intelligence-to-recruit-train-thousands-of-employees/
- Microsoft. (2017, January 9). *Microsoft and ICRISAT's Intelligent Cloud pilot for Agriculture in Andhra Pradesh increase crop yield for farmers*. Microsoft Stories. https://news.microsoft.com/en-in/microsoft-and-icrisats-intelligent-cloud-pilot-for-agriculture-in-andhra-pradesh-increase-crop-yield-for-farmers/
- Microsoft. (2017, November 7). *Digital agriculture: Farmers in India are using AI to increase crop yields*. Microsoft Stories. https://news.microsoft.com/en-in/features/ai-agriculture-icrisat-upl-india/
- Microsoft Azure Blog. (2019, October 8). *Democratizing agriculture intelligence: Introducing Azure FarmBeats*. Microsoft Azure. https://azure.microsoft.com/en-us/blog/democratizing-agriculture-intelligence-introducing-azure-farmbeats/
- Reger, G. M., Holloway, K. M., Candy, C., Rothbaum, B. O., Difede, J., Rizzo, A. S., & Gahm, G. A. (2011). Effectiveness of virtual reality exposure therapy for active duty soldiers in a military mental health clinic. *Journal of Traumatic Stress*, 24(1), 93–96. https://doi.org/10.1002/jts.20574
- Rio Tinto. (2018, January 30). *Rio Tinto's autonomous haul trucks achieve one billion tonne milestone*. https://

www.riotinto.com/en/news/releases/2018/ahs-one-billion-tonne-milestone

- Rio Tinto. (2024, May 27). *BHP and Rio Tinto collaborate on battery-electric haul truck trials in the Pilbara.* https://www.bhp.com/news/media-centre/releases/2024/05/bhp-and-rio-tinto-collaborate-on-battery-electric-haul-truck-trials-in-the-pilbara
- Rizzo, A. S., & Koenig, S. T. (2017). Is clinical virtual reality ready for primetime? *Neuropsychology*, 31(8), 877–899. https://doi.org/10.1037/neu0000405
- Sarda, S., Das, S., Roy, D., & Subramanian, V. (2020). Understanding digital mental health needs and usage with an artificial intelligence–led mental health app (Wysa) during the COVID-19 pandemic: Retrospective analysis. *JMIR Formative Research, 4*(1), e17294. https://doi.org/10.2196/17294
- Source.ag. (2024, May 28). *Source.ag expands into North America with AI solutions for growers*. Source.ag. https://www.source.ag/news/source-ag-expands-into-north-america-with-ai-solutions-for-growers
- Tesla. (n.d.). *Autopilot.* Tesla. https://www.tesla.com/support/autopilot
- United Parcel Service. (2022). *ORION: Optimizing delivery routes with AI.* https://www.roundtrip.ai/articles/ups-route-optimization-software
- VA News. (2023, September 28). Immersive technology assists with treatment for PTSD. https://news.va.gov/124160/immersive-technology-assists-treatment-for-ptsd/
- Vaswani, A., Shazeer, N., Parmar, N., Uszoreit, J., Jones, L., Gomez, A. N., ... & Polosukhin, I. (2017). *Attention is all you need.* Advances in Neural Information Processing Systems, 30, 5998–6008. https://arxiv.org/abs/1706.03762
- Verhoeven, P. (Director). (1997). *Starship Troopers* [Film]. Sony Pictures Releasing.

- Von Däniken, E. (1968). Chariots of the gods? Unsolved mysteries of the past. Souvenir Press.
- Vyasa, S. (2000). *Mahabharata* (C. Sharma, Trans.). Penguin Books.
- Wageningen University & Research. (2024). *Autonomous Greenhouse Challenge 4th edition*. WUR. https://www.wur.nl/en/research-results/research-institutes/plant-research/business-units/greenhouse-horticulture/show-greenhouse/autonomous-greenhouse-challenge-4th-edition.htm
- Weidinger, L., Mellor, J., Rauh, M., Griffin, C., Uesato, J., Huang, P.-S., ... & Gabriel, I. (2021). *Ethical and social risks of harm from language models*. arXiv preprint arXiv:2112.04359. https://arxiv.org/abs/2112.04359
- Witzel, M. (2012). The origins of the world's mythologies. Oxford University Press.
- Wysa. (2024, April 15). AI detects 82% of mental health app users in crisis, finds Wysa's global study released on the role of AI to detect and manage distress. https://blogs.wysa.io/blog/company-news/ai-detects-82-of-mental-health-app-users-in-crisis-finds-wysas-global-study-released-on-the-role-of-ai-to-detect-and-manage-distress
- Wysa. (n.d.). Wysa: Transforming mental health through AI-driven support. EMHIC. https://emhicglobal.com/case-studies/chatbots/wysa-transforming-mental-health-through-ai-driven-support/
- Zendesk. (2023). CX Trends Report 2023.

www.ingramcontent.com/pod-product-compliance
Lightning Source LLC
LaVergne TN
LVHW052313200926
848481LV00002B/552
* 9 7 9 8 2 3 1 5 8 9 1 1 1 *